BLACK & WHITE

written by: Dean Evans

Created by PRIMA GAMES UK
Published by PRIMA GAMES
A Division of PRIMA COMMUNICATIONS, INC.
3000 Lava Ridge Court
Roseville, CA 95661
(916) 787-7000
www.primagames.com

PRIMA GAMES UK
Publishing Director: Maryanne Booth
Product Manager: Ashley Young
Assistant Project Editor: Helen Woodey
Senior Designer: Sue Huntley
Designers: Josephine Jeffery and Laura MacGregor
Retail Services Manager: Sam Blanchard

Created in the United Kingdom
Printed in the United States of America

ISBN: 07615-3593-4
Library of Congress: 2001088359
01 02 03 04 DD 10 9 8 7 6 5 4 3 2 1

FOREWORD ▷

Black & White took over three years of hard work to make. At Lionhead Studios we always knew what we wanted, but getting there stretched us as far as we'd go. We wanted a game that looked, felt and played unlike any other. We wanted people to think about what they were doing, to decide how they'd play and to feel that this was a world in which they could do anything.

As we wrote the challenges and designed the quests, and as the threads of the story came together we knew we'd achieved everything we wanted to. We also knew that, while the game would be vastly rewarding to play, there would be so many ways of doing it and so many possible outcomes— no two people would ever play *Black & White* the same way.

Whether you play as a gracious goody or an almighty evil, this excellent Prima guide caters for all. It provides everything you'll need to know on how to become a well-worshiped and well-respected god of gods.

This Strategy Guide will not just lead you gently through the lands of Eden, it'll show you wonders, deliver oddities and explain the incredible. It'll give you an insight into how our minds work and, we hope, how *your* mind works. So not only will you find out who you really are, you'll also find out what's in that ravine, over that mountain or deep in those dark woods.

So enjoy what lies ahead. And whatever you do, look after your Creature. And remember; no matter how godlike you think *you* are, *he's* the most powerful being in the world.

Peter Molyneux,
and the Lionhead team.

CONTENTS

"Here's what you can expect to find in the rest of this guide. I found the Creature section most illuminating."

"Hey, there's nothing in here about us! I was promised at least ten pages all to myself. Get me my agent!"

CHAPTER 1
GETTING STARTED

"God moves in a mysterious way
His wonders to perform;
He plants his footsteps in the sea,
And rides upon the storm.

Deep in unfathomable mines
of never-failing skill,
He treasures up his
bright designs,
And works his
sovereign will."

William Cowper, 1774

WELCOME

There's no right way to play *Black & White*. Much of Lionhead's incredible god game is shaped by the way that you interact with the world of Eden, and the things that exist within it. Its strength is that it provides the kind of freedom most games never come close to. Will you rule as a benevolent deity? An evil overlord, perhaps? Or adopt a personal morality that lies somewhere between the two? It's your world, your choice. But whichever spiritual path you decide to take, Prima's Official Strategy Guide will not only help you be all-seeing and all-powerful, but all-knowing as well.

From an exploration of game mechanics to in-depth Creature details, throughout the following pages you'll find a wealth of information to help you get the most out of *Black & White*. You'll find a complete walkthrough of the game's Story Mode, plus tactics and strategies for the Multiplayer options. Check out the list of Miracles (and how best to use them), plus the most efficient way to maintain and expand your villages. In addition, there are detailed sections covering Disciples, godly combat and Creature care. However you play, consider Prima's Official Strategy Guide to be your third conscience, an extra voice alongside that beardy-bloke in the toga and the imp with attitude.

After all, even an almighty omnipotence needs a little help from time to time...

GAME OPTIONS AND LINKS

Black & White offers several different gaming options to suit all players—namely Story Mode, and multiplayer. But even though Story Mode is the default way of playing *Black & White*, you can explore this option entirely at your own pace. If you want to sit and gaze at the beautiful landscape as the sun sets, for example, you can do just that. Or zoom high above any of the five Lands to see the clouds forming and the weather patterns change. The Story Mode can even become a godly goldfish bowl, giving you plenty of time to develop small villages into sprawling towns, or play at length with your Creature.

The Story Mode
Black & White's default game mode comprises a series of interactive game tutorials. These form part of an evolving narrative which spans five different landscapes.

The God's Playground
More than just a stand-alone refresher course for inexperienced deities, The God's Playground transports you to an island where you can practise rock-hurling, tree-uprooting and general gameplay.

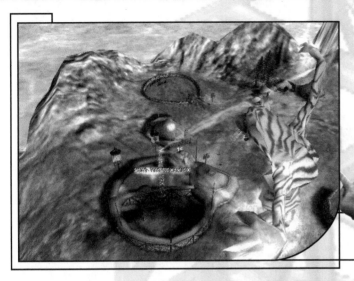

Skirmish mode provides a whole new adventure for your Creature.

Skirmish

All the fun of *Black & White's* expansionist gameplay, but without the evolving storyline. Test your divine powers by pitting them against one, two or three computer-controlled opponents. Bring your own Creature.

Multiplayer

Battle against other gods online in deathmatch and cooperative situations. This will surely be the ultimate test of your village management, Miracle-casting and Creature-controlling skills. Intense action.

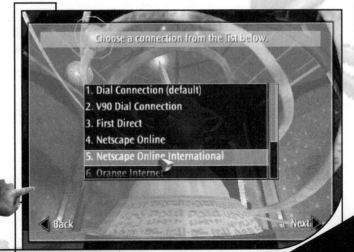

Choose a connection from the list below.

1. Dial Connection (default)
2. V90 Dial Connection
3. First Direct
4. Netscape Online
5. Netscape Online International
6. Orange Internet

◄ Back Next ►

Pit your skills against online opposition.

There's lots to find out online about the game.

Web Link—Lionhead

Get more information about Lionhead and play *Black & White* online by logging onto **www.lionhead.com** or **www.bwgame.com** respectively.

Web Link—Prima Games

For more information about Prima Games and its series of strategy guides, aim your Web browsers towards **www.primagames.com**.

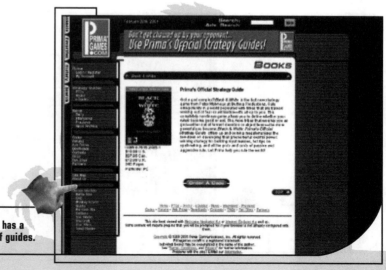

Primagames.com has a great selection of guides.

MASTERING THE CONTROLS

Although the tutorials in *Black & White* advocate total mouse-controlled movement, it's arguably more efficient to use both the mouse and keyboard during play. Special keyboard shortcuts and *Black & White's* handy Bookmarking feature enable you to soar, zoom and spin with absolute ease, leaving the mouse for interacting with characters and objects. Obviously, the following methods are only suggestions, but try them out and see which one you feel most comfortable with.

TIP

Placing Bookmarks is a useful way of moving around the landscape quickly.

Mouse Movement

If you opt for a combination of mouse and keyboard, you'll typically use the mouse to interact with any onscreen objects. Use it to cast Miracles, pick up or drop items, and to zoom to a point within your visual range (with a double-click of the left button). Press both mouse buttons (or use your mouse wheel if you have one) to zoom in and out on the landscape. Pressing both mouse buttons also enables you to rotate your viewpoint—simply move the mouse left/right rather than up/down. It's much easier than moving your godly hand to the edge of the screen.

keyboard controls

Rather than move using the "grabbing the landscape" technique, you may find it easier to scroll around the gameworld with the help of the cursor keys. In fact, the keyboard provides many handy shortcuts that total mouse control just can't provide. For example, hit the TAB key to jump to each of the Village Stores that you control (which means that you don't need to Bookmark any villages). Similarly, by pressing the CTRL and SHIFT keys you can quickly zoom into the hand-cursor location. Rotate the view using the Z and U keys, adjust the pitch with Q and A. Finally, use F4 to jump instantly inside your Temple.

Bookmarks

One of the most useful godly powers is *Black & White*'s Bookmarking feature, which enables you to Bookmark (or "tag") up to seven different important areas (such as fish shoals and forests) or people in a Land. You might want to devote CTRL and "7" to your Worship Site, for example, thereby enabling you to quickly check on your worshippers and their needs. (Pressing CTRL and "7" together will set the bookmark; pressing "7" on its own will then take you to your Worship Site.) Or you might want to replant scattered trees into a more accessible forest, or keep tabs on a shoal of fish so that you can periodically plunder it for food. You could also try tagging enemy held villages for quick and easy access. Delete a Bookmark at any time by pressing CTRL, SHIFT and the relevant number of that Bookmark.

THE GOD'S PLAYGROUND

Press F2 during a single-player game and you'll have the opportunity to take time out in The God's Playground. This sparsely populated island principally offers its visitors a refresher course in *Black & White's* control system— moving, rotating the view, zooming, and so on. It also gives you the chance to play around with a village without being threatened by an enemy or bogged down by part of a storyline. Here, you can practise Miracle-casting and village-building in complete, comfy safety.

The series of tutorials automatically starts when you arrive on the island, but you can quit them by pressing the ESC key, which leaves you free to tour the landscape. Quit The God's Playground completely by pressing the ESC key twice. The various tutorial lessons that you can expect to find, and the other features of this island, are detailed overleaf. Note that if you've played through and mastered the skills taught in Land One of the Story Mode, you'll learn nothing new here. You may, however, find it useful to practise using a Workshop and managing the small village to be found on this island.

You can learn all sorts of essential skills in The God's Playground. It's a safe place for you to experiment freely.

Try out new ideas with your village—you can practise your building skills and experiment with Miracle-casting.

The god's playground: tutorials

Task   Stalk the Island Keeper as he walks along a straight path.

Lesson How to rotate the view.

Task   Tail your teacher as he walks around the entire mountain path.

Task   Follow the Island Keeper as he walks around the entire mountain path (this must be completed in under five minutes).

Lesson Pitching the view.

Task   Use the pitch controls to keep the Island Keeper in sight as he walks up a pathway.

Task   Use the pitch controls to keep the Island Keeper in sight as he walks down a pathway.

Task   Trail the Island Keeper as he walks along a winding path, using all of the skills that you have now learned (i.e. move, rotate and pitch).

Lesson Zooming the view.

Task   Pick up the five giant teddy bears and put them in the nearby ditch.

Lesson   Picking up objects.

Lesson   Double-click the Move button to reach a destination.

map: the god's playground

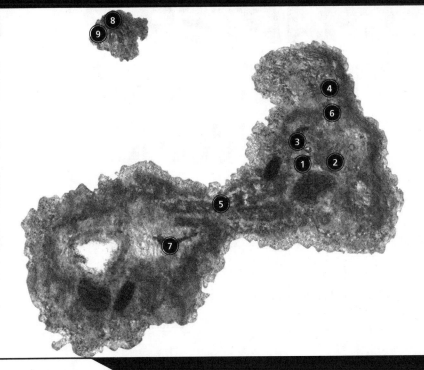

KEY: FEATURES
1: Village
2: One-shot Miracle Dispensers
3: Japanese Wonder
4: Celtic Wonder
5: Toy Ball
6: Skittles Set 1
7: Dice
8: Skittles Set 2
9: Toy Balls

CHAPTER 2
The Way of the World

"we've come a long, long way together,
through the hard times, and the good.
i have to celebrate you baby,
i have to praise you like i should..."

Fatboy Slim (Praise You)

WORLD MECHANICS

W hatever gaming mode you play, success in *Black & White* isn't just a case of who's got the biggest Temple. Like other real-time strategy titles, success relies on expanding your empire and juggling the natural resources available. How do you provide your villagers with enough food? Do you cautiously manage your forests, or chop them down quickly and dump the timber into storage? And then there's your Creature to consider. Do you teach your giant chimp to hurl Lightning Bolts at enemy villages? Or persuade your massive monkey to lug trees to the Village Workshop? Figure out how the *Black & White* world works and you'll better understand what you can do in it.

Nice Temple. Sea views and all!

Belief

In *Black & White*, knowledge isn't power. At least not on its own. In this game, your mightiness is determined by the amount of Belief the people have in you. The more Belief you generate in the game world, the more power and influence you gain as a result. So it doesn't matter whether you're a benevolent deity or a happily vengeful one, you always need villagers that believe in you in order to maintain your power. Success in *Black & White* boils down to keeping your villagers firmly tied to your own brand of virtual religion—whether you impress them with kindness, or rule through fear and Fireballs.

You'll need to gain the respect of your villagers to gain power.

influence

Although your Creature can act for you on any Land you play on, you can't rely on him entirely. Unfortunately, you can only interact with the environment within your own (or an ally's) sphere of Influence. These bubbles of power are focused around your Temple or the villages that you control, and their size depends on the level of Belief that you command. Operating within your own Influence, you can flex your godly muscles, move objects, cast Miracles and generally meddle with reality. Outside it, you can only soar and zoom, and your powers will quickly fade to nothing the further away you move from the people who brought you into being.

Flex those godly muscles with a few morning stretches.

It's worth remembering a simple set of rules, especially if you want to build your strength to fight rival divinities.

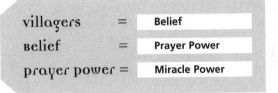

villagers	=	Belief
belief	=	Prayer Power
prayer power	=	Miracle Power

Admittedly, any villages you come across in *Black & White* will be able to cope without help from above. During the daylight hours, they auto-assign themselves various jobs according to the desires of the village. For example, if their settlement requires a large amount of food, you'll see many of the villagers involved in farming and fishing. But if new buildings are required, villagers take a break from their food-gathering chores to construct them, chopping down trees for timber if required.

"We plough the fields and scatter..."

Natural Resources

The Lands in *Black & White* feature any (or all) of the following resources. Some are vital in keeping your villages thriving (i.e. grain), while you can manipulate others to provide bonuses that will help you as you expand your tribal empire (i.e. Fireflies and rocks). The following pages detail what natural resources you can expect to find on a typical landscape and what (if anything) they're worth to your villagers.

FIELDS/GRAIN

You need to assign a Farmer Disciple to any bit of land you wish to keep active.

Left to their own devices, villagers only farm intensively when there's an increased desire for food at the Village Store. To keep the fields active, you need to assign a Farmer Disciple to them. The maximum yield you can expect from a single field is 350 Food. However, the maximum amount a Farmer can dig up and carry to the Village Store in one trip is 150 Food. New fields require four Scaffolds (see the Village Expansion section of this guide).

FISH

Fish are often to be found in shallow waters near easily-accessible beaches. The maximum amount a Fisherman can catch and carry home in one trip is 150 Food. So it's often easier (and more efficient) to Bookmark your nearest fishing grounds, and to catch fish by hand. In comparison to the dedicated Fishermen, you can grab up to 1,500 worth of fish providing the shoal is large enough. Note that fish stocks periodically disappear through over-fishing, but are replenished slowly over time.

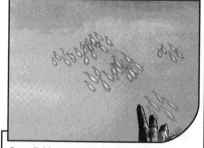

Over-fishing can exhaust stocks. Although they will be replenished.

SHEEP

Sheep are one of the four sources of meat that your villagers (and your Creature) can rely on. Watched over by self-proclaimed shepherds, these animals are periodically slaughtered to provide Food for the settlement. Dumping a sheep into the Village Store yourself adds around 850 Food to the existing stockpile. Use them, as and when required, for the creation of extra Food and as a sacrifice at the Worship Site to gain instant Prayer Power.

You can sacrifice sheep to gain instant Prayer Power. You can even sacrifice the shepherd if you like!

COWS

If cows are located close to a village you control, your villagers typically begin to manage any herd that they find. Expect to create 1,200 Food when you add a fully-grown heffer to supplies in the Village Store. Like the sheep, use cows as and when you need them, both for Food and as a sacrifice at the Worship Site to gain a boost to your Prayer Power.

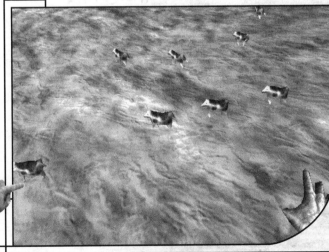

You can sacrifice cows too—horseradish anyone?

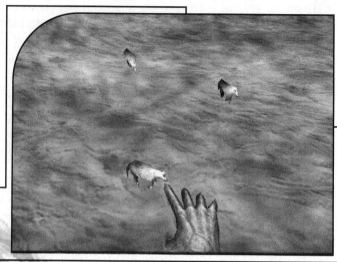

Like most animals, horses can be sacrificed or eaten.

HORSES

Like the cows mentioned previously, horses can be converted into 1,200 Food for your village. Typically found grazing on large, grassy plains, horses can also be sacrificed at a Temple's Worship Site to generate extra Prayer Power. Note: like most of the animals on the *Black & White* landscapes, you'll need to zoom in close to see them on lower detail levels.

PIGS

While pigs don't require the wide-open spaces demanded by cattle, sheep and horses, the return on them is somewhat disappointing. Typically, you should expect a pig to create around 290 units of Food when added to the Village Store. As with the other animals here, you can sacrifice pigs to provide Prayer Power when required.

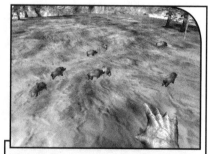

Little piggies can be sacrificed too. Zoom in to see what meat there is available.

TREES

Trees provide your only source of building materials in *Black & White*, and without a plentiful supply of Wood, you'll find it difficult to expand a village or repair any of its existing buildings. Consequently, you need to make best use of the resources you have around you; using Wood Stores wisely in the construction of core buildings such as extra houses, a Crèche, Graveyard, Wonder, plus handy One-shot Miracle Dispensers. Discover more about the buildings you can put up in the Village Expansion section of this guide.

A good few trees here. Now decide what you want to build with all that wood.

In the *Black & White* world, a tree is not just a tree. The amount of Wood that you can eke out of logged timber is obviously dependant on the size and type of tree it is. There are several species of tree in *Black & White*, all of which can be converted into Wood.

There's little point in identifying each individual tree (who looks closely when zooming around the world at 10,000 feet?) But the trees in *Black & White* can be divided into three distinct groups. Typically, trees with rounded foliage are worth the highest amount of Wood. These trees encompass the following types and are worth roughly the amounts indicated below:

Beech (700)
Birch (500)
Cedar (700)
Oak (800)
Olive (500)

How much wood is this little beauty worth?

TREES CONTINUED

Trees with a noticeably pyramidal shape (as shown) are worth substantially less than their rounder counterparts. Typically, these trees encompass the following types and are worth roughly the amounts indicated below:

Conifer (350)
Pine (350).

Lower down the scale of woody goodness, the **Palm (300)** can be put into the same category as the Pine and the Conifer above. You'll find this tree predominantly on

You can tell by the tops of these trees that they're less valuable in wood.

warmer landscapes (i.e. Land Three of the Story Mode), or near gently-sloping beach areas. You may also find the **Cypress (400)** here.

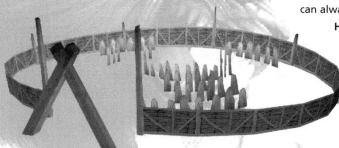

Finally, and if you're desperate for building materials, you can always uproot small **Bushes (15)** and larger **Hedges (100)** to bolster your timber supplies. Any **Fences (50)** that you have in your village can also be recycled and turned into fresh building materials—although the return is pitifully small.

Looks nice and tropical here. Take a little rest under one of these trees and think about what you'd like to build with them.

You'd be surprised what you can build with a couple of hedges, a bush or two and an old fence!

ROCKS

The rocks that litter the landscapes in *Black & White* fulfil a variety of functions. Most notably, you can use them as weapons—hurl one at an enemy village to dent its infrastructure and erode the villagers' Belief total. In addition, rocks placed deliberately near buildings in your villages attract Fireflies (see below), while dropping a boulder in the centre of town encourages your villagers to dance around it at dusk, slowly transforming it into an Artefact (see Village Expansion).

This could cause some damage, but where do you want to throw it?

RAIN/WATER

Unless you can create your own downpours to order with Water and Storm Miracles, rain falls randomly in the *Black & White* game world. Its most basic but vital function is to irrigate your fields—a good drenching makes your crops grow faster. You can also use Water to encourage the growth of new trees, to impress villagers with localised showers, and to put out any fires that start nearby.

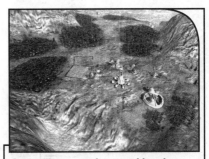

Some villagers are impressed by rain— they really should get out more often!

FIREFLIES

When night falls, Fireflies take to the air to loop and circle around objects on the ground. Uncover the daytime hiding place of one of these glowing bugs and you'll find it has often turned into a One-shot Miracle. Encourage Fireflies to make their home in your village by providing them with rocks or small bushes to escape under when the sun rises.

These little pretties like to hide under rocks and small bushes during the day.

ONE-SHOT MIRACLES

As mentioned earlier, you can often kickstart the development of a village by finding and using One-shot Miracles. These appear in many forms—from Wood (providing around 700 units of timber) and Food (conjuring up about 700 units of grain), to Heal, Water, Fireball, Storm and Shield Miracles.

The villagers

Arguably, your most important natural asset is the villager. These men and women are the source of your power—without them, you're quite literally nothing. In each settlement, villagers assume one of a number of different tasks: Farmer, Forester, Fisherman, etc., according to the desires of the village. We'll look at these specific jobs in the Using Disciples section later in this chapter. For now, it's important to know what makes each villager tick.

Pressing "S" reveals important bits of information about your villagers (pressing this key when your godly hand is over a single villager only displays the statistics of that particular inhabitant). If a villager has a name, this is displayed at the top, while below you'll find a description of what that person is currently doing, i.e. "Going to a building site", "Planting crop", and so on. The bottom line in these data-bubbles features three different attributes, i.e. A:20 L:91% F:64%. These are the Age, Life and Food statistics. Women may have an extra "P" statistic, indicating that they are pregnant. And if a villager is poisoned or sick, an "S" appears.

It's essential that your villagers believe in you.

VILLAGER: AGE

New villagers start off at the tender age of 1 and stay in the Crèche (if one has been built) until they reach maturity. Each villager ages 10-12 years during a typical day in the game world, and you should expect most of them to live beyond 75 years of age.

Kids grow up fast these days: by bed-time these nippers will be teenagers!

VILLAGER: LIFE

The harder a villager works, the faster his/her Life attribute falls. This percentage score represents how much life force or energy a villager has. When this value drops significantly, a villager automatically returns home (if available) and sleeps in order to replenish it. To restore the Life stat without letting villagers sleep, you can cast a Heal Miracle on any flagging souls. Note: villagers who have been called to the Worship Site will not automatically seek rest to replenish their Life scores. If you ignore their need for shut-eye and their Life scores drop to zero, they die.

Try to remember the mere little mortals. They'll need time to rest.

VILLAGER: FOOD

Each villager requires around 85 units of Food per game day in order to survive. Remember that villagers can only carry 150 units of Food back from the fields or fishing grounds. You will need to either increase the intensity of your farming or provide extra grub for your villagers to keep them satisfied.

There's nothing like a good supply of food to keep your villagers happy.

THE TEMPLE

𝕴n each Land in *Black & White*, your Temple remains the focus of your power. While a lack of Belief reduces the amount of power that you can wield, the loss of your Temple always consigns you to oblivion. You must do everything you can to ensure that it cannot be threatened.

Your Alignment (i.e. good, evil or somewhere in-between) and the extent of your Influence is reflected in the Temple's design and its overall size. On the outside, the Creature Pen is a permanent fixture at the front, while Worship Sites are added by the villagers of each settlement you impress and convert. You can zoom directly to your Temple from anywhere on a Land you're playing by tapping the Space Bar twice. Pressing the Space Bar twice again returns you to your earlier position. By pressing F4 you can jump directly into the World Room inside your Temple. Once inside your titanic tabernacle, game time in the world outside freezes. This enables you to browse through the information stored within the Temple's main rooms at your leisure.

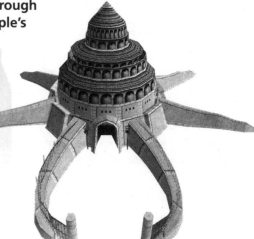

The chambers available to you are:
The World Room (F4),
The Creature Cave (F5),
The Challenge Room (F6),
The Save Game Room (F7),
The Options Room (F8) and
The Library (F9).
You can also visit an additional
room: The Future Room.

The World Room

This main chamber features two useful items. The first is a map of the Land you're currently playing, with toggles to show the range of your Influence, plus the location of any Temples, Creatures, Miracle activity or Silver Scroll challenges. You can jump to any part of the landscape by double-clicking on the map with the Move button.

The decor at deity HQ is suitably impressive.

On the wall between the Challenge and Save Game rooms, you'll find the World Room Scroll. This details the current world population, births/deaths, not to mention the number of buildings and disciples that you have in your empire. Unfortunately, this scroll only gives a general overview of the region under your control. If you have more than one village, you can't use it to see how many Farmer Disciples you have in one as opposed to the others. With so much to do in a typical *Black & White* game, you'll rarely spend time here.

The Creature Cave

Pressing F5 transports you to the Creature Cave, which contains a wealth of information about your Creature's abilities and development. We'll be looking at this room in more detail in the chapter entitled Creature Comforts.

Your Creature is so vain he plasters the walls of his cave with his own resumés.

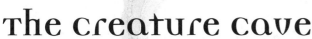

The challenge Room

Catch up on those Silver challenges.

Available in the Story Mode only, the Challenge Room enables you to keep track of any Silver Scroll challenges that you've clicked on. In certain cases, you can replay the introductory sequences for the challenges to remind you what you're supposed to be doing. All-seeing and all-knowing comes with practice, after all. The keyboard shortcut to this room is F6.

The save Game Room

Get to a good point—and save it!

As the focus of your godly power, it should come as no surprise that this is also where you can magically freeze your progress in Black & White and store it away for later use. More commonly known as the Save Game option, there are 21 slots available (although the top row is typically reserved for auto-saves). Quick-jump to this room by tapping F7.

The options Room

The Options Room gives you access to the same game-tweaking settings that you find by pressing ESC and choosing Options from the main menu. Of the four menus available, Controls is by far the most useful. Here you can redefine any of the keyboard shortcuts—you might want to change the key for Rotate Right to "X" instead of "U", for instance. Teleport here by hitting F8 in-game.

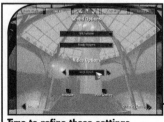

Time to refine those settings...

The Library

Through the pink door lies the Library, a one-stop refresher of all the information and tips given to you during the game. This archived Help feature is divided into the following categories: Controls Help, Village Help, Creature Help, Miracle Help, Did You Know? and Story History. You can also enter this room via the F9 window.

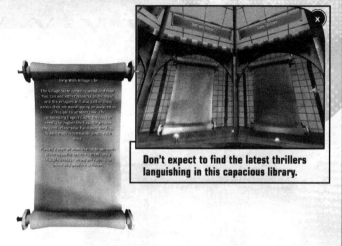

Don't expect to find the latest thrillers languishing in this capacious library.

The Future Room

There may not be much to the Future Room now, but this empty wing of your godly sanctuary is where Lionhead plan to install new game modules that will make *Black & White* even better. Pay regular visits to Lionhead's Website at **www.lionhead.com**, and you'll be the first to know when these expansions or plug-ins become available.

Ah, time to flex those divine digits and see what Lionhead has to offer...

VILLAGE MAINTENANCE

𝕴f a god is nothing without his people, then the people are nothing without their villages. In *Black & White*, you'll either be given a hamlet to call your own or you'll need to build one from scratch. How much time you get to develop your settlements depends on the sort of game you're playing. In the main Story Mode, you can play very much at your own pace. Get involved in a Skirmish, however, and it's a land-grab right from the start—you need to keep one eye on your enemies at all times. Whatever mode you play in, the ability to successfully expand and maintain your villages is a vital part of *Black & White*'s gameplay.

There are several different problems you need to face. A village must not only be able to support its existing inhabitants (generating Food and Wood for them), but it should also encourage population growth. Ideally, a village needs to be organised enough to function efficiently in your absence (i.e. while you manage other villages or tend to the needs of worshippers at your Worship Site). Left alone, your villagers should do their best to look after themselves, farming, fishing and chopping down trees when necessary. They even construct new buildings (albeit slowly). As their god, however, it's important that you give them a helping hand.

The building types available to you, and the different tasks that you can assign to your devout followers, are detailed over the next few pages.

In most of game scenarios, you start with a group of core structures—typically your Temple, a Village Centre, a Village Store and a Large Abode. Even if none of these structures exist, your villagers auto-build them for your first village, adding a Worship Site when they've finished. When you begin to expand your empire beyond this primary settlement, you'll need to rely on a Workshop to produce extra buildings. Your villagers auto-build a Workshop on Lands where appropriate.

Building Types

TEMPLE

scaffold cost: N/A
construction cost: 4,000 Wood
function: Ethereal Base, Divine Hideout, focus of godly power

Essential information: Remember that your hallowed Temple is the focus of your power—if it gets destroyed, you lose whatever game you're playing. Similarly, by vaporizing an enemy's Temple, you consign them to oblivion and remove them from the game. However, it should also be noted that when a Temple is attacked, it first distributes the damage it suffers between the other buildings that the defending god owns. With this in mind, you should convert or destroy all opposing villages before making any final attack on an enemy Temple.

Is this all the little worms can muster?

workshop

scaffold cost: 3 (7,500 Wood)
construction cost: 3,500 Wood
function: Produces Scaffolds

Essential information: The Workshop is vital in any game where you have to expand and attack an opponent. In most *Black & White* scenarios (apart from Land One and Two in the Story Mode), the Workshop comes as part of the basic village package, along with the Temple, Village Centre, Village Store and one free Abode. Supply a Workshop with 2,500 units of lumber and it obediently churns out a Scaffold. This is the building block from which all other structures are created. By combining Scaffolds together, you can construct everything from a two-man tent to a Miracle-enhancing Wonder.

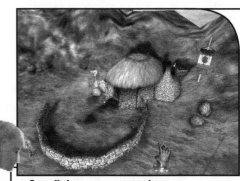

From little acorns, great oaks grow...

1 scaffold	Small Abode
2 scaffolds	Large Abode
3 scaffolds	Civic Building*
4 scaffolds	Field
5 scaffolds	Village Centre
6 scaffolds	Miracle Dispenser
7 scaffolds	Wonder

* Civic Building describes the Workshop, Graveyard, Village Store and Crèche facilities.

village centre

scaffold cost: 5 (12,500 Wood)
construction cost: 5,750 Wood
function: Village management/source of Influence

Essential information: While some settlements in *Black & White* can and do exist without a Village Centre, as a god you'll have no real influence over them. More than just a colossal monument to your almightiness, the Village Centre is an important indicator, showing just how much (or how little) a town believes in you, and what miraculous powers it can add to your own. Most importantly, without the Totem that forms the core of each Village Centre, you'll have no access to a Worship Site or those vital Miracles activated by it. The Village Centre is also a vital source of Influence, radiating a sphere of power that enables you to interact with the world beyond the immediate area surrounding your Temple.

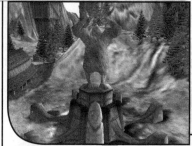
It's the little touches that mean so much.

scaffold cost: 1 (2,500 Wood)
construction cost: Varies
function: House

Essential information: Relatively quick and cheap to build, the Small Abode typically sleeps two. Its convenience, however, is offset by the fact that the Large Abodes can often provide more living space for slightly less overall investment. It's worth noting, however, that while different tribes have the same basic building types, they use different amounts of Wood to construct Abodes. For example, a two-man Norse hut costs around 1,450 Wood to construct from a single Scaffold. Compare this to an investment of 1,000 Wood for a comparable Indian tent.

Location, location,location...

Large Abode

scaffold cost: 2 (5,000 Wood)
construction cost: Varies
function: House

Now for something more desirable.

Essential information: The Large Abode is arguably the most efficient way to house your population, and your village won't expand unless the people have a place to live. While the initial outlay is steep (5,000 Wood for the Scaffolds, plus the extra construction costs), you have the opportunity to erect homes that have room for up to five villagers. Like the Small Abode, the cost of building a Large Abode varies according to the tribe building it. Choose the location of your planned Abode carefully—some Large Abodes only sleep a maximum of three. Having used two Scaffolds, you want accommodation that can house at least four of your tiny people.

scaffold cost: 4 (10,000 Wood)
construction cost: 2,000 Wood
function: Food source

Essential information: As the population of a village expands, it becomes more difficult to provide your citizens with enough Food. Hauling fish from the sea and using the Food Miracle only gets you so far. Ideally, you'd like to be able to let your villagers look after themselves while you wander the landscape strutting your godly stuff. Adding extra fields is one solution, and boosts a village's production capacity by 350 Food per Field. However, the investment cost (four Scaffolds = 10,000 Wood) is a high one, especially when both you and your Creature can cast Food directly into the Village Store. Sheep, cattle and pigs can also be used to supplement meagre resources (see World Mechanics, on page 18).

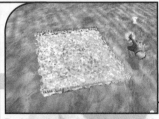
Tend your land well for better yields.

worship site

scaffold cost: 0
construction cost: 700 Wood
function: Prayer Power/
Miracle activation

Essential information: You can only
construct a Worship Site when you have a village
(complete with Village Centre) under your complete control. As an essential part
of the game, villagers auto-build this extension to your Temple—so you should
speed up the construction process by providing Food, Wood and dedicated
Builder Disciples. Only when a Worship Site is built do you have access to the
Miracles it provides. Its speedy construction should be your first priority. Without
a Worship Site, you lack Prayer Power. Without Prayer Power, you lack Miracles.
Without Miracles, you're weak.

When finished, the Worship Site features an altar (for making the odd sacrifice)
and displays the Miracles associated with the village that built it. You can directly
access Miracles by clicking on the icons here, although they require sufficient
Prayer Power before you can cast them. Miracles, Prayer Power, sacrifices and use
of the Village Centre Totem are examined in the section entitled Using Miracles.
Each time a new tribe is incorporated into your empire, an extra Worship Site is
added to your Temple (up to a maximum of six).

This megalith
should help
the hordes
worship the
best thing
about their
lives: you!

village store

Keep an eye on those flags!

scaffold cost: 3 (7,500 Wood)
construction cost: 4,000 Wood
function: Food and Wood storage

Essential information: The Village Store is one of three buildings that form the basic village infrastructure. More than just a medieval warehouse for Wood and Food, the Village Store is also an indicator for the needs of your village. These needs are expressed by the raising and lowering of Desire Flags. Thus, if the villagers are running short of food, the Food Desire Flag is hoisted up one of the six flagpoles on the store—the higher the Flag, the greater the need.

Village desires are also interlinked, so once you satisfy one need, another appears in its place. For example, provide enough Food and Wood for your villagers and they indicate their desire to expand their settlement by raising the Children Desire Flag. Create Breeder Disciples to satisfy this need and they then demand more buildings for the extra people to live in. More buildings equals more Wood, more people eat more Food, and so on. It's an endless cycle of moan-management, but by fulfiling village desires you encourage more Belief. The Desire Flags that can be raised are as follows:

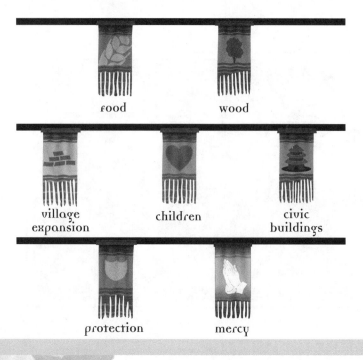

food

wood

village expansion

children

civic buildings

protection

mercy

crèche

scaffold cost: 3 (7,500 Wood)
construction cost: 2,000 Wood
function: Encourages birth of children

Without this, kids wander off.

Essential information: Each village you own should possess the full-range of Civic Buildings. The Crèche is one such municipal structure, an important addition to a growing settlement that encourages your citizens to have more children. Not only that, but kids born into a village with a Crèche stay safely in the Crèche until they reach maturity. Without one, the little ones simply follow their mothers, and are vulnerable to the attacks of wild animals and rival expansionist deities.

Graveyard

scaffold cost: 3 (7,500 Wood)
construction cost: 2,000 Wood
function: Avoids villagers mourning the dead

Essential information: At first, the Graveyard may not seem to be a key village building. But like the Crèche, it performs a vital function, reducing the degree of fuss caused when a villager shuffles off his or her mortal coil. Without a Graveyard, healthy villagers stop what they are doing to mourn a person who has died. It's an understandable reaction, but entirely inconvenient—especially if the death interrupts the sowing of new crops or the completion of an important building. The presence of a Graveyard simply removes the need for mourning, enabling the village to function normally despite the regular clog-popping of the old and the infirm.

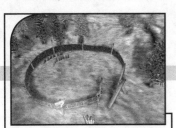
Graves stop your settlers mourning.

miracle dispenser

scaffold cost: 6 (15,000 Wood)
construction cost: 5,500 Wood
function: Provides one-shot Miracles

Essential information: If you've played the Story Mode beyond the intro, you'll have encountered the joys of One-shot Miracle Dispensers already. Should you have enough resources to enable you to combine six Scaffolds together, you can create your own Dispensers to order. You might want to have a Water Miracle on standby in case an enemy chucks Fireballs in your direction. Or you might want to line up a series of Lightning Bolt Miracles for use in a later attack. With a DIY Miracle Dispenser installed in your village, you can also harvest the Miracle One-shots that appear, snatching them up and storing them safely nearby for later use.

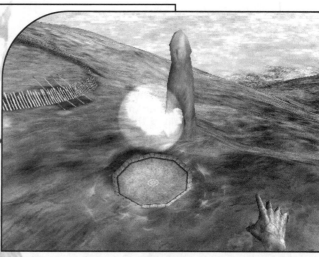

Miracle Dispensers are useful for all aspiring divinities.

wonder

scaffold cost: 7 (17,500 Wood)
construction cost:
10,000 Wood (approximately)
function: Enhances tribal powers

Bump up Belief by building a Wonder.

Essential information: Eight different tribes are featured in the *Black & White* game world, namely: Aztec, Celtic, Egyptian, Greek, Indian, Japanese, Norse and Tibetan. Each of these ancient races has unique strengths, and these are enhanced by the construction of a Wonder.

 Aztec Wonder—increases the power of aggressive Miracles, such as Fireballs. Each villager also worships harder.

 Celtic Wonder—increases the power of all resource-based Miracles, such as Wood or Food. Also increases the amount of Wood the villagers can obtain from from each tree.

 Egyptian Wonder—reduces the amount of damage your Creature takes. Reduces the Prayer cost of the Teleport miracle and boosts power of the Winged Creatures Miracle.

 Greek Wonder—increases the power of the Pack of Animals Miracle. Increases the birth-rate in allied villages.

 Indian Wonder—increases the power of Lightning Bolt Miracles and improves the speed at which villagers can move.

 Japanese Wonder—increases the power of all Healing Miracles and reduces the appetite for Food in villages.

 Norse Wonder—increases the yield from fish farms and increases the strength of weather Miracles, such as Water. Also reduces the Wood cost of village buildings.

 Tibetan Wonder—decreases the desires of all the people in the tribe. It also increases the strength of Shield Miracles.

VILLAGE EXPANSION

The more villagers that you have, the greater your powers can become. Why be satisfied with three huts and a Village Store, when your settlements can have a Graveyard, Crèche, Workshop and enough Abodes to accommodate three times the number of villagers? Village expansion isn't optional, it's inevitable. As you fulfil the basic needs of your citizens (i.e. Food and Wood), they then desire children, which in turn necessitates the construction of even more houses. As the population grows, the villagers also demand a full set of the civic buildings available in *Black & White*— Village Store, Workshop, Graveyard and Crèche.

Village expansion is inevitable. You must provide for your people.

Manage all these requests successfully and the population eventually thinks about building you a Wonder. If there's a basic aim in *Black & White,* it's to expand your sphere of Influence, dominate the landscape and defeat other gods. The construction of a Wonder and of One-shot Miracle Dispensers is vital in boosting your overall ethereal might. Raw materials permitting, there's no real limit to how far you can expand one village. It's much more effective, however, to create an empire of smaller settlements—either by converting neutral/enemy villages or by founding extra ones using a new Village Centre. See the Village Maintenance section for more information on building types and construction costs.

conservation & forestry

One of the biggest headaches you'll face when trying to expand a settlement is finding enough wood. The basic Wood Miracle can provide you with around 700 units per casting, but this costs you a substantial slice of your Prayer Power.

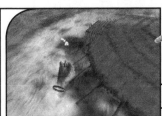

You can relocate your villagers to other villages.

The solution is to make best use of the trees that you have, investing wisely in civic buildings and houses, plus, where necessary, relocating villagers to settlements where there is free space. It may also help to replant the trees near you to make small forests. This ensures that the wood is easily accessible and that the trees can be watered to improve growth.

Try to keep your Village Store stocked up with Wood.

With the Workshop and the Village Store desperate for fresh timber, sooner or later your trees are going to run out. While there may be an abundance of bushes, these barely convert into 20 units of usable Wood. Fortunately, while it can be an effort to continually cast Wood Miracles yourself, you should be able to rely on your Creature to provide extra supplies. Of course, because he has his own personality, he probably won't summon lumber to order. If, however, you have shown him how to supply wood to buildings under construction, he will often cast a Wood Miracle to help out.

Lastly, the Forest Miracle can also be used to boost Wood levels. We will be talking more about this later on in the Using Miracles section.

The Forest Miracle is always an option if you're desperate for Wood.

Miracles seeds and Artefacts

The quest for "free" magic should also be high on your godly "To Do" list when expanding your village. Typically, as you grow a settlement, you will strip the surrounding area of trees and bushes. This deforestation will remove the natural hideyholes used by Fireflies during the day. You can encourage these luminescent critters back to your village by placing rocks randomly amongst the houses. Should Fireflies flit around your settlement after nightfall, they will have no other choice but to disappear beneath the rocks when day breaks. Lift the rocks each morning to check for the Miracle Seeds they turn into.

Another interesting by-product of scattering rocks around your village is that they may eventually be turned into Artefacts. Leave a boulder near the Village Centre and villagers may start to dance around it as the sun starts to go down. As the villagers continue to jig around the rock, they slowly imbue it with Prayer Power—much like the way the altar is charged up at a village's Worship Site. When sufficient power has been

Leave Rocks scattered around your village—you may get a pleasant surprise.

Impress your villagers with Artefacts and Wonders.

passed from your cavorting citizens to the Artefact, the boulder starts to glow in the player's colour. Building a Wonder next to an Artefact boosts the size and power of the finished building. You can also use an Artefact to impress another village; simply pick it up and drop it in the midst of the villagers you wish to convert.

impressing villagers

In addition to slowly expanding your home village, a key part of *Black & White*'s gameplay revolves around religiously invading other settlements. Rather than conquering other villages using massed ranks of spear-waving militiamen, *Black & White*'s heavenly (and hellish) generals need to direct an ongoing war of ideas and deeds. To take over a neutral settlement, you typically need to generate over 500 Belief points from the villagers there. A village held by a rival god has a significantly higher Belief total.

TIP

Building structures near another village impresses its inhabitants.

There are several ways that you can create Belief in a village that you wish to convert. People are naturally impressed by things that are beyond their understanding—the sight of a giant Creature, a bush flying through the air, rain falling from a cloudless sky. The bigger the population of a village, the quicker you can hope

You must create as much Belief as you can in your villages— More Belief means more power.

The more Wonders and Miracles that you perform, the more your village will thrive. You alone can shape its destiny.

to impress and convert it (i.e. there are more people to see the Wonders and Miracles that you perform). Create enough of an impression, and you can eventually overturn the Belief Needed total (displayed by holding the mouse over the Village Centre). Once you've done this, the village falls under your control and you can shape the destiny of its inhabitants.

Not only must you gain Belief in villages you *don't* yet control, you must also retain high Belief levels in those villages that you *do* own. The higher the Belief level in your home village, for example, the harder it will be for another god to convert it. The villagers in *Black & White*, however, are hard to please and you can't rely on repeating the same miraculous feat again and again to garner large chunks of Belief. The key to impressing a village is to use a varied mix of actions and Miracles, from throwing trees into the Village Store to casting a Physical Shield over the entire settlement.

On the following pages, you'll find some of the best ways to impress and convert villages (both neutral and enemy-held). Note: to maximise the effectiveness of your miraculous actions and magic, make sure that you play to a crowd. Creating a flock of birds is certainly impressive, but it won't help you much if only a few people see it. If an enemy-held village has a reduced population because the majority have been called to the Worship Site, attack their Village Centre to temporarily recall them.

USING SECRET AGENTS

Known more commonly as Missionaries, these villagers can be placed in a neutral or enemy-held settlement to impress and influence the populace. Admittedly, the Belief gained through Missionary action is small, but it can help as part of a campaign that also includes direct action by you and your Creature.

USING YOUR CREATURE

One of the most effective ways to impress a village is to use your Creature. Even when your Creature is a little on the diminutive side, a village's first glimpse of your magical beast is enough to generate some flabbergasted Belief from the inhabitants. The bigger your Creature, the more impressive villagers (including your own) will find him. So much so that it's a good idea to spend some time building up his strength, fitness and maturity on the early Lands in the Story Mode. This

The use of Missionaries can gain you Belief in opposing villages.

Your Creature can be used to perform many tasks.

> **TIP**
>
> The bigger and more impressive your Creature, the better the village reaction.

ensures that you're well-prepared for the war of attrition to come. If you have access to the Enlarge Creature Miracle, use this when your Creature is in a village you wish to convert.

Better still, if you have taught your Creature how to throw trees and food into a Village Store, he can impress the villagers with his talents. If you're following a darker path, getting your Creature to kick down a village building certainly turns a few heads. Finally, if your Creature has learnt to cast any of the Miracles that you've encountered, he can employ these to gain chunky wedges of Belief. Water, Food and Wood Miracles are always impressive, while Heal and the Shield Miracles also get a good response. To focus your Creature's attention on a settlement, tie him to the Village Centre with the Leash of Compassion or the Leash of Aggression.

USING YOUR GODLY POWERS

There are several things that you can do personally to gain Belief in a neutral or enemy-controlled village:

1. Supply the Village Store with any raw materials that it lacks. Check the Desire Flags and provide Food or Wood accordingly. If they require extra buildings, try giving them a Scaffold from your Workshop.

2. You don't even need to supply extra resources. Just try manipulating those already available. Picking up and dropping Food and Wood from the Village Store will even gain you some Belief.

3. Pick up and throw objects through the village. Rocks have a tendency to damage the buildings, but trees, bushes and even animals impress the crowds as they fly across the sky.

4. If you can reach right into the village, try throwing its villagers around. Don't throw them too far—you don't want to accidentally kill the very people you need to impress. Placing villagers on rooftops is also impressive.

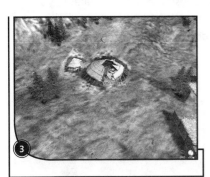

1. Villagers are impressed by your organisational and technical skills when you build structures close to them. In essence, they see a rival village doing better than they are and think: "I want some of that." Cue Belief gain.

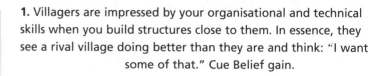

2. Attacking a village is a sure-fire way to get a response. Hurl rocks at their Village Store, set fire to their Workshop, fire Lightning Bolts at their houses (particularly impressive if used in short, ineffective bursts).

3. In a scam only a god could get away with, try attacking a village (i.e. aiming a Fireball at a house), then help to put the fire out (with a Water Miracle) and provide Wood to repair the damage. You'll get Belief for all three actions.

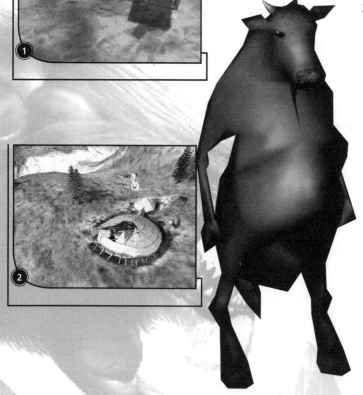

4. We mentioned the Artefact earlier in this section, and by placing a charged-up rock in an opposing or neutral village, you can gain valuable chunks of positive Belief.

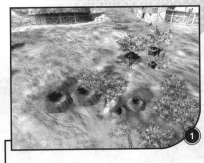

1. Try uprooting trees and bushes around the target settlement to search for One-shot Miracle Seeds. Using these enables you to conserve the Prayer Power you've stored at your Temple.

2. If your sphere of Influence doesn't enable you to directly interact within the boundaries of a village, you can impress its inhabitants from afar. Bushes seem to have the most aerodynamic properties.

3. Bar the Fireball, Water, Food, Wood and Heal Miracles, there are a number of other spells that get a good response. These include: Spiritual and Physical Shields, Storm, plus the supremely effective Winged Creatures Miracle.

4. Remember: tree-throwing, Miracle-casting and the activities of your Creature count for nothing if a rival god puts up a protective Spiritual Shield. As long as it stands, the villagers won't be impressed by anything you do.

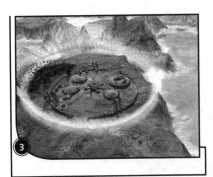

USING DISCIPLES

Brainwashing your villagers into becoming Disciples is a key management strategy in any *Black & White* village. In fact, you'll be fortunate to have real control over any settlement that doesn't have Farmer, Breeder and Builder Disciples lurking in its midst. The *Black & White* game engine has been finely balanced so that your villages automatically look after themselves, but independence isn't the same as invention. Only by using Disciples strategically can you encourage the growth of your empire.

Designating Disciples is a simple matter of dropping a villager next to a job that you wish them to do. These "chosen ones" subsequently do their allotted task, pausing only to eat and sleep when their L (Life) and F (Food) statistics fall dangerously low. They then continue to obediently serve, until you relieve them of their duty, reassign them, or they fall over and die. It's a hard life, but they toil night and day for the greater good. Or the greater evil, depending on your point of view. Keep periodic tabs on the well-being of your Disciples by pressing the "S" key to display their key attributes.

Disciples also ignore the call to worship at the Worship Site, enabling a village to tick over when most of the populace are away. Disciples only travel to the Worship Site if the Totem is raised to the 100 percent level.

farmer Disciple

Planting Crop
A:24 L:99% F:81%

Drop him in the field
and watch him sow
his oats.

To activate: Drop villager in a field
preferred gender: Female

Essential information: Farmer Disciples won't just farm
the one field that you assign them to. Brainwashed to
love farming, these guys plant crops in any field that
doesn't already have food growing in it. If a field does
have an existing crop, the Farmer Disciple will begin to
harvest it—however, this only happens when the crops
are ripe (maximum yield 350 Food). He/she then carries
the harvested crop (albeit 150 units at a time) to the
Village Store.

To make best use of your Farmer Disciples, choose only
female villagers to work the fields. Having a male Breeder
Disciple in the village ensures that population growth can
continue, even when most citizens are called to the Worship
Site. Farmer Disciples will become tired quickly if they're forced
to walk long distances carrying crops. Although you can't often
choose the location of your fields, you can shorten the journeys of
Farmer Disciples by adding Teleport gateways (if available to you). Note,
however, that maintaining Teleport Miracles requires constant worship at
the Worship Site.

forester Disciple

Chopping Tree
A:28 L:96% F:74%

This Disciple likes nothing better than making logs.

To activate: Drop villager near a tree
preferred gender: Either

Essential information: Designate a villager to be a Forester and they long to sing songs and write epic poetry about the joys of endless logging. Forester Disciples always attempt to cut down the nearest tree, unless that tree happens to be one deliberately placed in your village for aesthetic purposes. Like the Farmer Disciples, the fanatical focus of the Forester means that eventually they have to walk long distances to find the nearest supply of lumber. Again, Teleport Miracles can shorten journeys.

In the long run, however, it's debatable whether Foresters actually make that much of an impact. Considering your godly talents, you can actually process trees into Wood much faster than an army of Disciples ever could. You can also add supplies to the Village Store with the Wood Miracle and create new mini-forests with the aptly-named Forest Miracle. Take all this into account and you may find that you don't need a dedicated Forester at all. Note, however, that Foresters also carry leftover Wood supplies scattered around your village to the Village Store.

fisherman Disciple

To activate: Drop villager on seashore
(near fish shoals)
preferred gender: Either

Essential information: Fishing is another way to supplement the food gained from the fields. In areas where fish are plentiful, villagers automatically produce fishing rods and head for the seashore. A Fisherman Disciple makes fishing his sole raison d'être, pausing only to eat and sleep. He or she typically hooks 150 units of fish before returning to the Village Store with his or her catch. But like the Forester and the Farmer, the Fisherman Disciple is often faced with long walks to and from the resource that they plunder.

Frankly, the task that the Fisherman Disciple performs can actually be done quicker and more efficiently by your good or evil self. Fishing a large shoal of fish, a god can typically grab up to 1,500-worth of fish from the ocean in one go—the equivalent of ten trips for a lowly Fisherman Disciple. The most effective method seems to be to Bookmark a nearby shoal and then to transfer them all to the Village Store. The number of fish will rise again as time passes in the gameworld, enabling you to busy yourself with other tasks while the depleted stocks are replenished.

TIP

You can scare fish by clicking the Move Button near them.

Fishing
A:36 L:99% F:82%

The sun, the sea and the thrill of the catch.

Breeder Disciple

To activate: Drop male villager next to a female villager (and vice versa)

preferred gender: Male

Essential information: As the game points out on one of its loading screens: "Create Breeder Disciples to enlarge your population. But be aware—women can only get pregnant once in nine months. A man can breed constantly throughout this time." How much more of a hint do you need?

Young males make the most efficient Breeder Disciples. Watch the movement of these lusty villagers and you'll see that they will "Have Sex" with every available woman that they meet—although not every coupling will result in a pregnancy. Breeder Disciples are best dropped near the Village Store, because this is the building that most villagers visit regularly. When a woman becomes pregnant, a "P" is added to the trio of statistics on view when you press "S". The nine-month term then passes in a few minutes, adding a one-year-old kid to the village population. One Breeder Disciple, if he's young enough, can significantly boost a village's population, but only if there is sufficient space for new arrivals to live in. By making the majority of your other Disciples female, a male Breeder can continue to do his work even when most villagers are fanatically praying at the Worship Site.

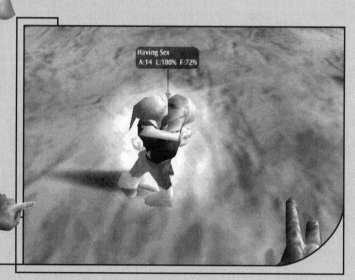

Having Sex
A:14 L:100% F:72%

The ultimate in divine voyeurism!

Builder Disciple

Building
A:15 L:94% F:86%

Zoom Out

"Hey, you—build me a decent citadel!"

To activate: Drop villager next to a new or damaged building
Preferred gender: Either

Essential information: You'll notice when you expand a village in *Black & White* that villagers often drop what they're doing to help in the construction of new buildings. A building site requires three main elements: willing builders, Food for the workforce, and sufficient Wood to complete construction of the planned structure. If there isn't enough Wood around to use, villagers go to the Village Store or nearby trees to get some. Similarly, if there isn't any grub to feed the eager workers, they need to stop and trudge to the Village Store to get more.

Arguably, the most efficient way to quickly erect new structures is to designate one or more Builder Disciples and to provide all the raw materials that they need for the job. The number of Builder Disciples that you assign depends on the size or the number of new buildings required. Like other Disciples, Builders work single-mindedly at their task, but still need to pause to get Wood and Food. If you deliver both these vital resources to the building site, however, Disciples have no need to leave and therefore complete the job quicker. Builders who have nothing to do (i.e. no new structures to build) congregate at the Village Centre. Builders also automatically start repairing damaged buildings.

missionary Disciple

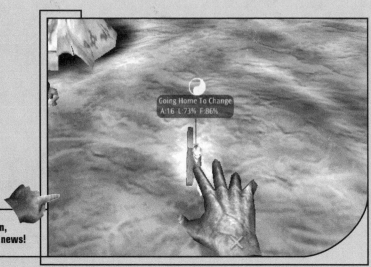

Go forth, my son,
and spread the news!

Going Home To Change
A:16 L:73% F:86%

To activate: Drop villager near an uncontrolled building
preferred gender: Either

Essential information: Missionaries can be extremely useful when you want to start converting a new village, but don't want to divert all of your attention to the task. True, gods are supposed to be all-seeing and all-knowing, but in *Black & White* you have one monitor and one view. Missionary Disciples are tools that can help you gain Belief in several places at the same time.

A Missionary effectively becomes a member of the village that you want to control, spreading word of your powers as he goes. However, this process only gains small chunks of Belief, much like digging a large hole with a small spoon. You can add extra Disciples to increase your presence, but it's a bit like adding extra spoons to dig the same large hole. Your Creature is the best way to impress villages if you don't want to do it yourself; Missionaries are best left to convert neutral villages. Use them in opposing settlements with a strong level of Belief, and you risk them being converted by the god you're trying to kill. For these reasons, it's a good idea to make your Missionaries male. You don't want to endanger your females, because they're the key to expanding your own population.

craftsman disciple

To activate: Drop villager next to a Workshop
preferred gender: Either

Essential information: The Craftsman Disciple lives only to lug supplies of Wood to the Workshop. Think of him as the Workshop's very own Forester Disciple. As such, Craftsman Disciples will encounter the same problems as their lumberjack counterparts—although this devoted servant doesn't have as far to trudge between the Workshop and the Village Store.

Again, while the Craftsman fulfils a useful role, it's debatable whether having a full-time tree-shifter is a good use of your resources. Not only can your disembodied hand process trees for the Village Store much faster than a Forester, you can do things that Disciples can't, such as transfer bulk shipments of Wood from other Village Stores, recycle fences, and so on. Furthermore, with a bank of Prayer Power at your disposal, you can build Scaffolds (using Wood Miracles) to order whenever you need them. Considering that a Craftsman can only transport around 250 Wood per trip, it takes a long time for them to amass the 2,500 units needed for just one Scaffold. You'll have conquered the world in the time it takes them to provide the materials needed to build even an extra house.

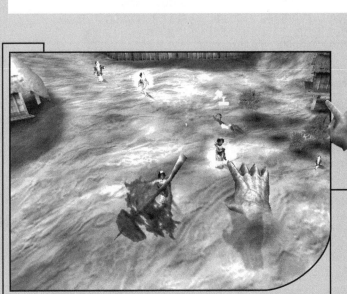

Carrying trees has its uses, you know.

Trader Disciple

"Come on, ladies, you know it's a bargain!"

To activate: Drop villager next to an uncontrolled Village Store
preferred gender: Either

Essential information: The Trader Disciple can be used much like a Missionary to impress a neutral village or one controlled by another god. Essentially, dropping a villager next to another Village Store instructs them to supply it with resources in the hope of gaining both Belief and Influence. Like the Missionary Disciple, this enables you to begin converting a nearby village while you strengthen your ineffable grip on your existing empire.

A Trader is only useful if the village you wish to impress has Desire Flags raised over the Village Store. Seeing a need for Wood, for example, a Trader Disciple attempts to rectify the situation by providing the raw material requested. Unfortunately, rather than chop down a nearby tree, the Trader returns to his home village to get the Wood he needs. For impressing a village within easy walking distance, this isn't much of a problem. But typically, the long trek between villages on some maps means that this method is a slow one. Note that the Trader can carry 500 units of Wood or Food at any one time. A Trader Disciple continues to supply a village after it's been converted.

Disciples At Work

The best way to use Disciples in a typical village naturally varies according to your strategies. You might want to build new structures quickly by designating a squad of villagers as Builder Disciples, for example. Your ideal quota of Farmers should be determined by the number of fields and your settlement's population—remember that one Disciple can work multiple farms. In a village that has six fields and a population of 15, for instance, you could assign the following number of Disciples:

Creating Disciples is a full-time job...

Farmer Disciples:	3 (Female)
Fisherman Disciples:	0
Forester Disciples:	1 (Female)
Breeder Disciples:	1 (Male)
Craftsman Disciples:	0
Builder Disciples:	1 (Female)
Missionary Disciples:	As and when required (Male)
Trader Disciples:	As and when required (Male)

The reasoning behind this is fairly straightforward. By making all of the Disciples (except the Breeder) female, you ensure that there are always women available in the village for the Breeder to pester—especially when villagers are called to the Worship Site. The number of Builders that you employ depends on how many core structures you start with, and how many you need to build to improve the efficiency of the settlement (i.e. Crèche, Graveyard).

shepherds

While not strictly a Disciple's position, you'll notice that full-time shepherding duties are assigned to villagers as a village expands. Whether they herd cattle, sheep or pigs, the basic routine remains the same. The Shepherds watch the animals, keep them together, and periodically slaughter them to provide food for the Village Store. You can't directly assign a villager to become a Shepherd—there's no provision to do so in the game. The Shepherd is used

The Shepherds look after the cloven-footed animals in the Village's care.

simply to keep animals from straying all over the map, gathering them together so that they are easily accessible to the godly player.

when animals attack!

It's worth noting that on some maps you may encounter wild animals that will attack straying villagers. For the most part, you need to keep an eye out for wolves. These roam in small packs and, while they mostly operate at night, can often strike right into the heart of frontier settlements. On Land Two of the Story Mode, for example, the threat is increased to include wild mountain lions and tigers. Don't waste any of your magical energy dealing with these

Wild wolves, lions and tigers can pick off straggling villagers if you're not careful.

ferocious attackers. When they stray within your Influence, pick them up and hurl them across the gameworld.

CHAPTER 3
It's a Kind of Magic

"unless you see signs and wonders, you will by no means believe"

Book of John, Chapter 4 Verse 48

USING MIRACLES

lthough *Black & White's* extraordinary Creatures tend to grab most of the attention, Miracles and the way that you use them are just as important. Miracles, and the unleashing thereof, are what being a god is all about. From resource-based magics to those that can literally shake the landscape, there are 22 unique Miracles that you can attempt to access. These Miracles can be cast by both you and your Creature, giving you the opportunity to form a devastating partnership as you battle for control of the various maps.

As we've mentioned throughout this strategy guide, the people are the ultimate source of your power in *Black & White.* Even if you decide to play as an evil deity, you still need the loyal worship of your followers to charge up the Miracles available to you. And the more villages you control, the wider the array of Miracles you can cast. Playing *Black & White* is a constant balancing act of short-term strategic goals (i.e. empire expansion) and a more long-term objective (the destruction of an opposing god). Whether you want access to the Heal Miracle to revive tiring villagers or the Mega Blast to attack an enemy village, most Miracles run on pure, unrefined "people-power". One-shots are the exception.

The worship site

Without a Worship Site, you'll have no access to any of the Miracles displayed on the Village Centre. Fortunately, once you have gained control of a settlement, its inhabitants will auto-build one for you. Unfortunately, they don't build it very quickly and there can be a long delay between conquering a village and being able to use the Miracle knowledge that it possesses—especially if your new acquisition is halfway across the map from your Temple. You can speed up the construction process by hand-delivering the villagers who trek across the landscape to build the new Worship Site. The Teleport Miracle is another useful way of shortening the journey. Cast it (if available) outside the target village before you begin converting it.

It can take a long time for the inhabitants of a village to build you a Worship Site.

The village totem

Even with a completed Worship Site, Miracles still need to be charged up with Prayer Power from your villagers. By raising and lowering the Totem in each Village Centre, you can adjust the number of villagers who make the pilgrimage to the Temple to charge up your Miracles. Send too many, and there will be nobody left behind to harvest food, chop down trees or expand the population. Dispatch too few, however, and your Miracles will take longer to become active—the smaller the crowd of worshippers, the less Prayer Power that's produced.

Strike a balance by designating Disciples to look after the village (see Village Expansion), and send the majority of your people to the Temple. Provide Food and Healing where necessary, or lower the Totem after a while to let the fanatical worshippers recover.

Send villagers to the Worship Site by raising and lowering the village Totem.

miracle types

On the following pages, you'll find a rundown of all the Miracles featured in *Black & White*, including information on whether they can be powered up, how much Prayer Power they cost to cast, and how best to use them. The Miracles here are split into two categories: General (these can be cast by both the player and Creature) and Creature (Miracles that have a specific effect on Creatures, i.e. Freeze.) Miracles are cast using the Action button and can be selected via the Temple and Village Centre, or via the appropriate Miracle gesture.

GENERAL MIRACLES

S food

Prayer Power cost: 7,000
Power-ups: Food Miracle Increase

Essential information: The Food Miracle doesn't require much in the way of explanation. Once selected and charged, it generates a limited-use Horn of Plenty, a food-crammed container from which you can pour around 710 units of nosh. Relatively cheap to cast, the Food Miracle is vital for delivering emergency supplies wherever they are needed, i.e. the Worship Site. If used in conjunction with the Aztec Wonder, the Food Miracle benefits from a boost that delivers almost twice the amount of food.

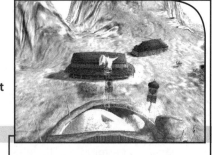

WOOD

Prayer Power cost: 7,000

Power ups: None

Essential information: Along with the Food and Water Miracles, the Wood Miracle is one of the most basic powers, yet also one of the most useful. Once cast and suitably charged, it can generate a maximum of 710 units of Wood anywhere within your Influence.

fOREST

Prayer Power cost: 13,000

Power-ups: None

Essential information: As its name suggests, the Forest Miracle creates an area filled with new trees. What you get for your Prayer Power is one large central tree surrounded by several smaller ones. Admittedly, it sounds like the perfect solution to wood shortage problems. Unfortunately, the Forest Miracle is only a temporary magical effect, and the existence of the trees needs to be maintained by the Prayer Power of your worshippers. You can quickly uproot and dump the new trees in the Village Store after casting. But the Forest-generated trees barely convert to more than 2,000 units of Wood. To get a decent return, you need to let the trees grow. But as the Miracle is temporary, you run the risk of losing the Forest as your Prayer Power level drops.

WATER
Prayer Power cost: 5,000
Power-ups: Water Miracle Increase

Essential information: As one of the first Miracles you are introduced to in *Black & White*, the Water Miracle is quick to charge and equally speedy to unleash. It's primarily useful for watering the crops in your fields, but also performs an Emergency Services role in putting out fires started by Fireballs and lightning strikes. The Water Miracle can be upgraded by one level (summoning a bigger cloud and more rain), but only if you have constructed the Celtic Wonder in the village where the Miracle is located. If your Creature masters this Miracle, he can use it to tend to crops in your absence and to quickly put himself out if he catches fire during a battle.

STORM
Prayer Power cost: 8,000
Power-ups: Storm Miracle Increase, Storm Miracle Extreme

Essential information: The Storm Miracle can be used both as a defensive ground-drencher (for putting out fires) and as an offensive magical weapon (for attacking and impressing other villages). In its bog-standard incarnation, the Storm produces a large, sprawling cloud that releases heavy rain over an area that you specify—this Miracle (like the two Shield Miracles) is activated by tracing a casting circle with the mouse. Powered up by a Norse Wonder, the Storm Miracle becomes the Storm Miracle Increase, adding lightning to its thundery mix. The second level power-up (Storm Miracle Extreme) combines rain, lightning and a violent tornado to produce some dramatic, area-effect sorcery.

HEAL

Prayer Power cost: 6,000

Power-ups: Heal Miracle Increase

Essential information: The Heal Miracle tends to be widely and immediately available on every game map, and it is a vital power if you want to keep hardworking (and hard-praying) villagers healthy and happy. Cast amongst a crowd of people, the Heal Miracle has a small area of effect and essentially boosts a villager's Life statistic, replacing the need for sleep. The Heal Miracle can only be powered-up once (via the Japanese Wonder), whereupon the healing zone it covers is widened. Like many of the Miracles featured here, casting the Heal Miracle also gains you increased Belief from villagers.

SPIRITUAL SHIELD

Prayer Power cost: 7,000

Power-ups: None

Essential information: Like the Physical Shield, Forest and Teleport Miracles, the Spiritual Shield, once cast, requires constant Prayer Power to maintain its integrity. Activated via a casting circle, the bigger the Shield the more Prayer

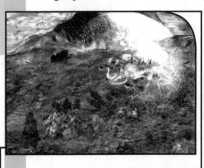

Power is required to anchor it in place. Villagers will not be impressed by another god's actions if they are safely within the pearlescent dome of a Spiritual Shield. Linked to the Tibetan tribe (who will often have this Miracle as standard), you shouldn't expect to power a Spiritual Shield for long. It's best used as a temporary measure to stop an attacking god, while you reply with a counterstrike that's designed to draw the expansionist deity away.

PHYSICAL SHIELD
Prayer Power cost: 7,000
Power-ups: None

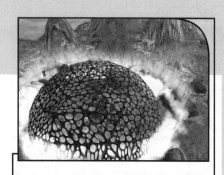

Essential information: Lessons in casting both the Spiritual and Physical Shields are part of the Story Mode on Land Two. It's important to know how to use these Miracles effectively, as summoned Shields tend to be slightly smaller than the casting circle that you trace. Consequently, it's worth designating a slightly bigger area than you actually need, just to make sure that the Shield protects what you want it to. While the Spiritual Shield screens your population from the effects of impressive Miracles, the Physical version provides some defence against rocks that are thrown at you. No power-up applies to either of the Miracle Shields.

WINGED CREATURES
Prayer Power cost: 12,000
Power-ups: None

Essential information: While most Miracles tend to impress watching villagers, most are designed to fulfil a vital function, i.e. the provision of food or water, the ability to heal, and so on. In contrast, the Winged Creatures Miracle is a pretty spell, designed purely to impress a village's inhabitants and to gain Belief in large, desirable chunks. Once charged, the Winged Creatures Miracle releases a flight of doves (good alignment) or bats (evil alignment) from the casting point. After casting, the Winged Creatures will fly away from the camera view. Like most Miracles, this one works best when unleashed in front of a crowd. Don't expect to gain many "ooh"s and "ahh"s of Belief if there are only a couple of Farmers to see it.

PACK OF ANIMALS

Prayer Power cost: 14,000

Power-ups: None

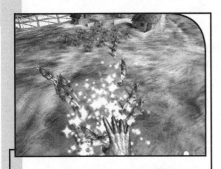

Essential information: The Pack of Animals Miracle is essentially a ground-based version of the Winged Creatures Miracle. Like the previous Miracle, Pack of Animals summons an impressive horde of wild beasts which will run away from the camera after casting. The only difference between this spell and the Winged Creatures Miracle is the fact that the animals may turn on the villagers they have impressed. If you plan to let loose the Miracle in the centre of a village, pay close attention to the aftermath. Of course, if you are trying to convert a neutral or enemy-controlled settlement, a little villager wastage is often unavoidable.

TELEPORT

Prayer Power cost: 5,000

Power-ups: None

Essential information: The Teleport Miracle provides an enticing benefit but at an inconvenient cost. The miniature vortices produced by the Miracle can shorten the distances between villagers, or quickly link villagers with hard-to-reach natural resources. The Teleport is also useful for providing villagers with a quick route to their Worship Site at your Temple—especially if the village is located some distance away. The downside to these swirling pink gateways is that you need to cast the Teleport Miracle twice (once for the entrance, and again for the exit) and supply constant Prayer Power to maintain them. Both villagers and your Creature will be able to make use of Teleports, and they can also be picked up and moved (i.e. recast) if needed.

FIREBALL
Prayer Power cost: 3,500
Power-ups: Fireball Miracle Increase, Fireball Miracle Extreme

TIP
You can put out fires using the Water or Storm Miracles.

Essential information: The Fireball can quickly become one of a god's main weapons—so much damage from such a tiny ball of flame. The Fireball's strength is that it causes collateral damage, setting alight anything made of wood that it comes into contact with: houses, civic buildings, whole forests, etc. To use the Miracle successfully, you need to master how much weight to put behind your throws. Too much, and it will soar over your intended target. Too little, and it will skid harmlessly along the ground. In some cases, moving the mouse after casting will apply Aftertouch and slightly alter the direction of the flaming missile. More importantly, by bringing an Aztec tribe into your empire, you have the ability to build an Aztec Wonder. This magical folly will power-up the basic Miracle into three- and five-Fireball variants.

You must put exactly the right amount of weight behind your throws.

LIGHTNING BOLT

Prayer Power cost: 5,000

Power-ups: Lightning Bolt Miracle Increase, Lightning Bolt Miracle Extreme

Essential information: For aeons, the Lightning Bolt has been a god's favourite Miracle. Just as this heavenly electricity was available to Zeus, it's also available to you in three devastating packages. The basic Lightning Bolt unleashes stabbing fingers of energy in front of the god that casts it. Hold down the Action button and you can focus the crackling power towards a single point, i.e. a building. Tap the Action button, however, and you can fire off quick bursts of Lightning at multiple targets while causing little real damage. The latter method is useful for when you wish to impress a village with a lightshow rather than set fire to it. There are two powered-up versions of the Lightning Bolt offering increased electrical power. Invest in an Aztec Wonder.

MEGA BLAST

Prayer Power cost: 16,000

Power-ups: Mega Blast Miracle Increase, Mega Blast Miracle Extreme

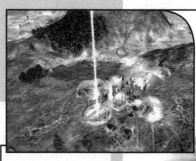

Essential information: As the most destructive of all *Black & White* Miracles, opportunities to use the Mega Blast are often few and far between. Play the last land in the Story Mode, and Nemesis will unleash the Mega Blast Miracle Extreme (five focused beams of energy) in an attempt to stop you reaching his Temple. It's an awesome sight, a pure shaft of power that explodes whatever it touches. Destructive deities might like to know that the Mega Blast can be powered-up twice by the construction of an Aztec Wonder. It's the perfect way to wipe an enemy off the game map.

FREEZE
Prayer Power cost: Varies
Power-ups: None

Essential information: This is an especially useful Miracle if you want to gain an advantage over an enemy with a slightly stronger Creature. By activating the Miracle on an enemy's Creature, you encase the beast in a bodysuit of ice. You then have a short while to operate without your rival's interference. It may just give you the opportunity that you need to take a strategic village, or rebuild a shattered settlement.

ENLARGE
Prayer Power cost: 7,000
Power-ups: None

Essential information: The sheer size of your Creature can gain Belief from any villagers who see it—the bigger the Creature, the larger the Belief gained. Ideally, you should spend time developing your beast on the early and relatively safe Story Mode lands. But for a quick fix, the Enlarge Creature Miracle allows you to temporarily boost your Creature's tonnage. Try casting it just before you try impressing a new village.

STRENGTH

Prayer Power cost: 8,000
Power-ups: None

Essential information: The Strength Miracle is one of five different powers that can be cast when two Creatures are involved in a battle. As you'd expect, by tracing the Strength gesture on the ground (without holding the mouse buttons down) you can temporarily boost the mightiness of your beast. The stronger you can make him, the more damage he can do when he strikes his opponent.

WEAKNESS

Prayer Power cost: 8,000
Power-ups: None

Essential information: As the opposite to the Strength Miracle, this is another Miracle that can be cast during the heat of Creature conflict. Naturally, when aimed at an opponent it will not only reduce his offensive power but will also affect how much damage he takes. When your beast is locked in a magical punch-up, take care that you don't accidentally cast the Miracle on your own Creature.

INVISIBLE
Prayer Power cost: 9,000
Power-ups: None

Essential information: While fully-grown Creatures are certainly powerful, they are hardly the most stealthy beasts and its difficult to sneak up on an enemy village without tipping off the god that owns it. This Miracle is an attempt to add a little covert action to the *Black & White* gameplay, allowing you to render your Creature almost invisible for a short period of time. Note that the magical sparkle that surrounds your Creature can still be seen.

COMPASSION
Prayer Power cost: 6,000
Power-ups: None

Essential information: Like its name suggests, the Compassion Miracle forces a Creature to be kind and nice no matter what Leash he is attached to. Like the Shrink and Freeze Miracles mentioned earlier, this magical power enables you to deflect an angry attack from an opponent's Creature. It might save your buildings from getting a kicking, but not for very long.

CHAPTER 3: IT'S A KIND OF MAGIC

AGGRESSION

Prayer Power cost: 6,000
Power-ups: None

Essential information: The Aggression Miracle is the direct opposite of the Compassion spell above. This one, however, is perhaps more useful, as when it is cast upon a Creature he will become angry with everything around him—even his own villages. If you can manage to cast this Miracle on an enemy Creature while he stands in one of his own settlements, you can force him to inflict damage on his own empire.

HOLY FLIES

Prayer Power cost: 8,000
Power-ups: None

Essential information: Like the Freeze Miracle, the Holy Flies spell is designed to stop a Creature from doing anything for a short space of time. Where the Freeze Miracle turned Creatures into ice-statues, Holy Flies afflicts them with an itchiness that they just have to scratch. Creatures will be preoccupied with their temporary skin disease until the Miracle fades.

GODLY COMBAT

As every *Black & White* map pits god against god in a battle for the hearts and minds of the villagers that live there, it won't be long before you clash directly with another expansionist omnipotence. To fight another god is to battle against their Influence on the landscape and the Belief that people have in them. Without these, your enemy is nothing.

While, as a god, you are really little more than a disembodied hand and a watchful eye, you do have a "body" that can be attacked and damaged. This is your Temple, not only the focus of your power, but the last bastion of your very existence. You need to do everything that you can to protect it from attack. To this end, you can use all of the Miracles available to you, as well as objects scattered around the landscape. While Creature Combat (detailed in the next chapter) is a traditional one-on-one melee, godly combat can be aimed at enemy villages, their inhabitants, and even the enemy Creature. When you are forced to defend yourself, or just want to flex your ethereal pecs, try some of the tactics on the following pages.

It's essential that you learn how to defend yourself. You may well be a god, but that doesn't mean you're invincible.

rock-throwing

Rocks don't cost you anything to deploy and can be extremely effective when aimed successfully. Use them to damage opposing buildings—this should focus your enemy's attention in the village that you are attacking, giving you space to attack another target. In games against the computer AI, you'll find that an opponent will quickly erect Physical Shields to protect a threatened settlement. As these cost Prayer Power to maintain, it means that the enemy's casting options are limited. Finally, keep rocks at a safe distance from your borders. The last thing you want is for your opponent to use his "virtual Influence" to steal your precious ammunition.

Look after your rocks. They have many purposes, one of which is clouting people on the back of the head!

one-shot miracles

Like the boulder bombs recommended above, One-shot Miracles can also be used to attack an opposing god's villages and Creature. Again, whenever you unearth a One-shot Miracle Seed, make sure that you store it far away from your borders. Leave them too close to your opponent's sphere of Influence and he may be able to steal them. Of course, this tactic works both ways.

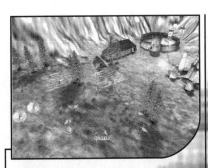

A Miracle Dispenser will give out One-shot Miraculous Wonders when it's fully charged.

scorched earth policy

To attack gods is to strike at the things that are most important to them. If you have Fireball Miracles active in your arsenal of powers, try hurling a few with the intention of setting fire to your opponent's forests. Wood is a vital resource in *Black & White*, and without sufficient natural resources, a god will be forced to rely on Miracles and Creature-assistance for his lumber. Note: although Fireballs can be immensely destructive, it's possible for a god to catch one before it hits the ground and throw it back.

flaming missiles

In a variation on the Fireball attack mentioned above, you might also want to try setting fire to a group of trees and throwing them at an enemy village or Creature. Admittedly, trees aren't aerodynamically suited for throwing, but this method gives you a number of flaming objects rather than one Fireball. Similarly, by placing boulders in the middle of a forest and then setting light to the trees, you can heat up the rock until it glows orange. These can then be thrown at the enemy to not only flatten buildings, but also to set them alight. Creatures can catch fire too, so throwing this type of hot-rock at your opponent's beast can also be very effective—that is unless the god has taught the Creature how to play "catch"...

Flatten buildings AND set them on fire!

Diversionary Attacks

By widening your strategy, you may find it useful to attack or impress more than one village simultaneously. For example, you can use Missionary Disciples in one settlement, send your Creature to another one, while you concentrate on a third. This will pose your opponent with something of a problem as he'll need to decide which of his villages he can defend. If you employ either the Scorched Earth tactic or indulge in a little rock-throwing, you can often keep an opponent distracted while you work to expand your Influence and Belief elsewhere.

Why not attack or impress more than one village at a time.

shields

It's fairly easy to pick up a rock and throw it at your opponent's village, but you should expect an enemy to do the same to you. Because your borders are fragile, you need to get worshippers to the Worship Site at your Temple as quickly as possible. With stored Prayer Power you can erect temporary Physical and Spiritual Shields to deflect long-distance attacks, or use your Miracles to retaliate in the hope that striking your opponent as he attacks you will force him to stop and repair the damage. You can deprive a god of Prayer Power by directly attacking one of his Village Centres which immediately recalls the worshippers from the Temple.

Don't think you can't be punished with a taste of your own medicine—other gods are often just as powerful as you are.

The Really wild show

Anything goes in godly combat and so nothing should be beneath you when it comes to protecting or expanding your Influence. Alongside hurled rocks (superheated or otherwise) and other miraculous bombardments, you can also use nature to your advantage. If you have come across any wild animals on your travels (i.e. Lions, Tigers, Wolves), you can sneakily pick one up and, should you be close enough, let it loose in an opponent's village. Unless the opposing god is looking closely at the settlement or has pressed the "S" button to show villager Statistics, they may not spot villagers being eaten alive!

creature power

As your empire expands, the role of your Creature begins to change. At the beginning of a map, he is used mostly to convert new villages and to supply existing settlements with resources. Once this set-up phase is over you may want to use him in a variety of ways. You might want him to guard your frontier, perhaps? Or to raid and attack an enemy village before the opposing god can respond? You might also keep him locked in

a series of battles with the opposing Creature, thereby cancelling the two Creatures out. Teach him some offensive spells (such as Fireball and Lightning Bolt) and you'll have a mobile deathbringer that can operate anywhere on the map. The big question you need to answer is: where do I need my Creature most?

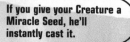

If you give your Creature a Miracle Seed, he'll instantly cast it.

CHAPTER 4
Creature Comforts

"I turned to speak to god, about the world's despair, but to make matters worse, I found god wasn't there."

Robert Frost, American Poet

WHICH CREATURE?

When you first play *Black & White*, you can choose to adopt one of three different magical Creatures: a cow, an ape and a tiger. Is one of these necessarily better than the other? It's difficult to make a real judgement—the cow is described as a "strong and noble beast", the ape is "intelligent and quick to learn", while the tiger is "fierce and lethal". While most Creatures in the game have a similar level of intelligence, their hidden characteristics can differ quite significantly.

There is a choice of three Creatures at the start of the game, but there are another 13 to command thereafter.

Although your initial choice of Creature is limited to the three mentioned above, there are actually 13 extra animals that can be found as you play through the game. Some of these, such as the wolf and the polar bear, are made available to you as rewards for completing Silver Scroll challenges in the Story Mode. We've taken care to point these out in the walkthrough where appropriate. The remaining Creatures can be unlocked by visiting the Creature Breeder on the first and fourth Lands of the Story Mode. But only if you have obtained the special Creature CD (available from selected retail stores). With this expansion disc and by solving the Silver challenges in the game itself, you'll be able to swap your Creature for any of those that appear on the following pages.

CHAPTER 4: CREATURE COMFORTS

creature statistics

In this chapter, we aim to show you the subtle differences between the 16 Creatures available in *Black & White*. Here, we've chosen to roughly compare a number of key Creature details:

- The number of minutes it takes for a Creature to reach maximum size. Note: Although minutes to maximum size are given, each Creature's growth rate is influenced by what and how much he eats, how much exercise he does and how much sleep he gets.
- A Creature's initial Strength rating.
- The number of minutes it takes for them to become strong from holding something heavy (i.e. a rock)
- A Creature's initial walking and running speeds.
- A Creature's reaction speed.
- The number of times you need to demonstrate a task before a Creature will learn it.

"I quite like the look of the horse. Or maybe the tortoise. Oh, there are so many fantastic Creatures to choose from."

"Why not the rhino? Ooh, or the gorilla? No, no, the brown bear. Or the polar bear? Hey, can we have two?"

Of course, the type of Creature you choose needs to suit the way you play the game. If you prefer launching your Creature into battle at every opportunity then perhaps a strong beast like the wolf would be suitable. However, if you want an intelligent Creature which can look after your villages while you fight in person, then the ape or the chimp is ideal.

In the rest of the chapter we'll be taking a look at what you should train your Creature to do (and not do) first; how to act good and evil; and what to do when you eventually get dragged into Creature combat. But first, let's parade the Creatures...

Ape

Essential information: The description of the ape that is given to you by the consciences ("intelligent and quick to learn") is completely accurate. The ape is the brainiest of the 17 Creatures here, and consequently he'll pick up new tasks and learn Miracles quicker than any other beast. You'd expect a trade-off for this high IQ, and the ape duly suffers with a low Strength value. Yes, you can train your simian to become a lean, mean fighting machine over time, but he's never going to be quite as adept at combat as the lion, gorilla and tiger. Note that both the ape and the chimp reach maximum size faster than any other Creature.

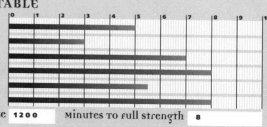

The ape is available at the start of the game. He's got plenty of brains but very little brawn.

SPECIFICATION TABLE

	0	1	2	3	4	5	6	7	8	9	10
Initial Fatness											
Initial Strength											
Initial Walking Speed											
Initial Running Speed											
Reaction Rating											
Intelligence Rating											

Minutes to Maximum Size **1200**   Minutes to Full Strength **8**

COW

Essential information: There are very few reasons why you should choose the unremarkable cow as your Creature. Carrying a little excess weight, this vegetarian monster weighs in with middle-of-the-road statistics in every category bar Strength— where it rivals the sheep and the tortoise in its scariness. But perhaps this average set of scores *is* the attraction; a Creature that will test your gaming skills further than one which is weighted to have high intelligence or good fighting skills. Note that the cow is also a slow-developer—1500 minutes equals 25 hours.

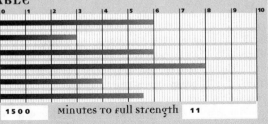

The cow's an average beast to start with, but in time he'll be as strong as the best of them.

SPECIFICATION TABLE

	0	1	2	3	4	5	6	7	8	9	10
Initial fatness											
Initial strength											
Initial walking speed											
Initial running speed											
Reaction rating											
Intelligence rating											

Minutes to maximum size: **1500**   Minutes to full strength: **11**

tiger

Essential information: Although it's a skinny animal when you first encounter it, the tiger will quickly bulk up when you've taught it to eat the right food. Where this Creature scores highly is in its physical characteristics—it's fast, strong and quick to react to its surroundings. With all this emphasis on strength and speed, the tiger does come up short in the brain department. It's not stupid by any stretch of the imagination, but you should expect it to take slightly longer to teach this Creature new Miracles and actions. For example, you may have to demonstrate the Water Miracle four times, when the ape will have it sussed after two.

The tiger's a slow learner but he makes up for it by being sleek, strong and fast.

CHAPTER 4: CREATURE COMFORTS

SPECIFICATION TABLE

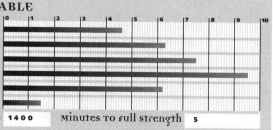

	0	1	2	3	4	5	6	7	8	9	10
Initial Fatness											
Initial Strength											
Initial Walking Speed											
Initial Running Speed											
Reaction Rating											
Intelligence Rating											

Minutes to Maximum Size	1400	Minutes to Full Strength	5

Leopard

Essential information: *Black & White's* big cats all have similar statistics, favouring physical prowess over brain power. While the leopard is slightly weaker than the tiger (at least to begin with), it's faster and more agile. The leopard's Reaction rating, which measures how quickly a Creature can spot something, turn towards it and accelerate, is the highest of all the beasts on show here. The leopard may have to stay behind after Miracle lessons for extra tuition, but he can develop into a top-class Creature.

Not the brightest Creature but one of the fastest.

SPECIFICATION TABLE

	0	1	2	3	4	5	6	7	8	9	10
Initial Fatness											
Initial Strength											
Initial Walking Speed											
Initial Running Speed											
Reaction Rating											
Intelligence Rating											

Minutes to Maximum Size	1450	Minutes to Full Strength	6

wolf

Essential information: The wolf is the evildoer's Creature of choice, a good all-round animal that boasts all the agility of a tiger and at least some of the intelligence of an ape. Fast, lean and strong, the wolf cuts a menacing figure on the landscape. The trade-off in abilities is a swap of reaction time for brainpower, so you'll find that it will take less time for the wolf to learn the basic Miracles (Food, Wood and Water), or get his head round looking after your Village Stores. If you get the opportunity to swap your Creature for this cunning alternative, you won't be disappointed.

The wolf is a good choice for evil players.

CHAPTER 4: CREATURE COMFORTS

SPECIFICATION TABLE

	0	1	2	3	4	5	6	7	8	9	10
Initial fatness											
Initial strength											
Initial walking speed											
Initial running speed											
Reaction Rating											
Intelligence Rating											

Minutes to maximum size	1300	Minutes to full strength	7

Lion

Essential information: As the king of the beasts, the lion combines good physical characteristics (speed and strength), with the sort of brainpower that you associate with an ape or a chimp. With the lion, you get the best of all worlds, which is why you won't find it on any of the early lands in the Story Mode. You'll need to wait until Land Five, where it is the reward for completing the appropriately-named lion Puzzle. By then, your Creature should have mastered most of the Miracles that you have across, so perhaps you won't need the lion's impressive reasoning power.

The king of Creatures but you have to work hard to find it.

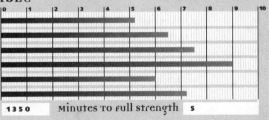

SPECIFICATION TABLE

	0	1	2	3	4	5	6	7	8	9	10
Initial Fatness											
Initial Strength											
Initial Walking Speed											
Initial Running Speed											
Reaction Rating											
Intelligence Rating											

Minutes to Maximum Size **1350**   Minutes to Full Strength **5**

Horse

Essential information: As a rule, horses aren't generally tough, scary animals with a talent for violence. But what this giant nag brings to the *Black & White* party is speed and above-average intelligence. Again, like most of the animals in the game, you can develop their strength (and so their fighting skills) through a programme of rock-lifting and throwing. The horse, however, isn't naturally strong, so you will need to maintain his exercises to avoid a drop in his statistics.

Work the horse hard to build up its strength.

SPECIFICATION TABLE

	0	1	2	3	4	5	6	7	8	9	10
Initial fatness											
Initial strength											
Initial walking speed											
Initial Running speed											
Reaction Rating											
Intelligence Rating											

Minutes to maximum size	1350	Minutes to full strength	8

tortoise

Essential information: Smart, yet slow and somewhat weak, you'll come across the tortoise when you reach Land Two of the Story Mode. Besieged god Khazar has chosen this popular pet as his own Creature, despite the fact that it takes a long time to grow in size, has slow reactions and wouldn't scare an opponent if you gave it a machine gun. What it does have, however, is an IQ to match the knuckle-dragging simians, plus a slightly higher tolerance to attack-based damage. It doesn't just wear that shell for decorative purposes, you know.

The tortoise is intelligent and well protected, but it's not likely to scare off its attackers.

SPECIFICATION TABLE

	0	1	2	3	4	5	6	7	8	9	10
Initial Fatness											
Initial Strength											
Initial Walking Speed											
Initial Running Speed											
Reaction Rating											
Intelligence Rating											

Minutes to maximum size **2000**   Minutes to full strength **12**

zebra

Essential information: You'd expect the zebra to have much the same basic qualities as the horse, and it does. Bar the exotic skin patterns, the zebra balances out its initial lack of strength with good speed and above-average brainpower. When running (double-click the Action button when on a Leash), this Creature can cover huge distances in a relatively short space of time. And like the other Creatures, its weaker characteristics can be improved over time with intense bouts of training.

A fast mover, but you'll need to build up its strength.

SPECIFICATION TABLE

	0	1	2	3	4	5	6	7	8	9	10
Initial Fatness											
Initial Strength											
Initial Walking Speed											
Initial Running Speed											
Reaction Rating											
Intelligence Rating											

Minutes to Maximum size `1300`   Minutes to Full Strength `8`

Brown Bear

Essential information: The brown bear combines strength and toughness with a reasonable degree of speed (especially for such a lumbering Creature). If you picked an ape as your Creature on Land One, you'll first encounter this grizzly giant as the Creature Guide. This is an indication of just how big and impressive the bear can grow. Admittedly, it will take him slightly longer to pick up new actions and Miracles. But as *Black & White's* Creatures don't differ wildly in their overall stats, this shouldn't be too much of an inconvenience in the long-run.

An impressive Creature and one you'll meet early on in the game.

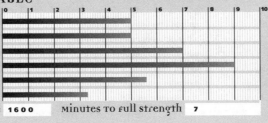

SPECIFICATION TABLE

	0	1	2	3	4	5	6	7	8	9	10
Initial Fatness											
Initial Strength											
Initial Walking Speed											
Initial Running Speed											
Reaction Rating											
Intelligence Rating											

Minutes to Maximum Size **1600**   Minutes to Full Strength **7**

93

polar bear

Essential information: The polar bear becomes available to you on Land Five, but only if you complete the Explorers Silver Scroll challenge on the first land. There's little difference between this Creature and the brown bear mentioned earlier. With decent all-round statistics, the polar bear doesn't have a real weakness—it's strong, intelligent, and surprisingly quick over the landscape for a big fella. Again, as *Black & White's* Creatures don't differ wildly in their mathematical genetics, whatever beast you start with can eventually be transformed into a rampaging titan.

A strong Creature that's only available in Land Five.

SPECIFICATION TABLE

	0	1	2	3	4	5	6	7	8	9	10
Initial Fatness											
Initial Strength											
Initial Walking Speed											
Initial Running Speed											
Reaction Rating											
Intelligence Rating											

Minutes to maximum size: 1650   Minutes to full strength: 7

sheep

Essential information: Can you strike terror into the hearts of men and beasts with a sheep? Not to begin with, no. As you'll see, the sheep has a tendency to become a little tubby, and it lacks the natural strength and blistering pace of a predator like the wolf or tiger. As it's not a natural fighter, it has slightly higher intelligence than the big cats. Should you choose this woolly companion, you'll have a lot of work to do if you want to shape it into a more terrifying attacker. But then, isn't this exactly what *Black & White* is about? Think of it as a challenge.

The sheep is the ultimate test for your godly skills.

SPECIFICATION TABLE

	0	1	2	3	4	5	6	7	8	9	10
Initial Fatness											
Initial Strength											
Initial Walking Speed											
Initial Running Speed											
Reaction Rating											
Intelligence Rating											

Minutes to Maximum size **1375**   Minutes to Full strength **13**

chimp

Essential information: Like the ape (one of three Creatures you can choose from in the Story Mode), the chimp isn't naturally built for combat. Rather than a bruiser, it's a more of a thinker, boasting a level of intelligence that makes it quick to learn new things. Its other basic characteristics can be lumped into the "average" category, although strength and endurance can be improved over time. Reasonably speedy, the chimp can easily become a fantastic all-round Creature. It looks particularly impressive in its evil incarnation, by the way.

The chimp is impressive in its evil guise.

SPECIFICATION TABLE

	0	1	2	3	4	5	6	7	8	9	10
Initial Fatness											
Initial Strength											
Initial Walking Speed											
Initial Running Speed											
Reaction Rating											
Intelligence Rating											

Minutes to Maximum Size	1190	Minutes to Full Strength	9

ogre

Essential information: You'll first encounter the ogre on Land One, where the tiny "Sleg" stubbornly guards a Heal Miracle Increase Dispenser. The much bigger, meaner "son of Sleg" (complete with Gremlin army) skulks with purpose on Land Four. In both cases, the Slegs are not difficult to defeat and boast an average array of stats and characteristics.

Note: The ogre cannot be used as a Creature, but you will need to know how to defeat it. For combat tips and details, see the Creature Combat section later in this chapter.

You'll first encounter the ogre on Land One.

SPECIFICATION TABLE

	0	1	2	3	4	5	6	7	8	9	10
initial fatness											
initial strength											
initial walking speed											
initial running speed											
reaction rating											
intelligence rating											

minutes to maximum size 1400   minutes to full strength 6

mandrill

Essential information: A strange monkey variant, the mandrill provides yet another all-round Creature for you to choose. Blessed with an average set of statistics, the mandrill isn't as intelligent as its simian relations—thus you'll need to show him new things four or five times before he'll pick them up. It's worth noting that the mandrill, chimp and the ape take much less time to grow to full size than most Creatures. The mandrill, for example, reaches full size in around 21 hours of gameplay. In comparison, the tortoise won't grow to full size for almost 34 hours.

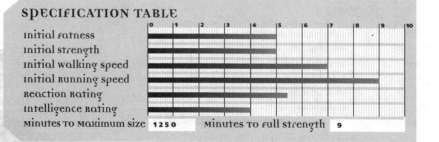

The mandrill grows quickly in size but is a slow learner.

SPECIFICATION TABLE

	0	1	2	3	4	5	6	7	8	9	10
Initial fatness											
Initial strength											
Initial walking speed											
Initial running speed											
Reaction rating											
Intelligence rating											

Minutes to maximum size **1250**   Minutes to full strength **9**

Rhino

Essential information: Big and somewhat stupid, the heavily-armoured rhino is one of the more menacing of *Black & White's* Creatures. In fact, it boasts one of the lowest intelligence levels in the game. So while it may be big and strong, the rhino isn't the sharpest tool in the shed. Again, this simply means that the rhino will take longer to pick up new actions and Miracles. But once taught, this bulky beast will easily be a match for any other Creature it might face. Note: the rhino won't grow to maximum size for around 32 hours.

A menacing beast who grows slowly in size.

SPECIFICATION TABLE

	0	1	2	3	4	5	6	7	8	9	10
Initial fatness											
Initial strength											
Initial walking speed											
Initial running speed											
Reaction rating											
Intelligence rating											

Minutes to maximum size	1900	Minutes to full strength	8

gorilla

Essential information: As you might expect, the gorilla resembles the ape, chimp and mandrill in many key respects. It is, however, a much tubbier Creature, stronger and "bigger-boned" than its tree-swinging cousins. You might even venture to say "fat". As usual, there's a trade-off and the gorilla gains its extra initial strength at the expense of intelligence. Nevertheless, this Creature is a good option for gods who wish to pursue an aggressive, slightly more evil approach to their people-management. Watch the gorilla's weight—the fatter it gets, the slower it'll move.

The gorilla is another good choice for evil players.

SPECIFICATION TABLE

	0	1	2	3	4	5	6	7	8	9	10
Initial fatness											
Initial strength											
Initial walking speed											
Initial running speed											
Reaction rating											
Intelligence rating											

Minutes to maximum size	1300	Minutes to full strength	7

CREATURE TRAINING

The Creature facts and stats on show in the previous section are a useful indication of a beast's basic characteristics. But that's all that they are. In *Black & White*, you can shape your Creature very much in your own image and its personality (and looks) will change as a result. So, if you pursue a strategy of sweetness and light, your Creature will be directly affected by the caring way that you interact with the world. Consequently, it will try to approach things with the same compassion. Its appearance will also be transformed—the skin will lighten in colour and the features will soften.

Your Creature's appearance is a direct reflection of your actions—train him well.

If you prefer to follow a dark path, then similarly your actions within the gameworld will be mimicked to a certain extent by your Creature. Attempt to convert a village by destroying a building or two and your Creature will regard it as normal village-influencing tactics. Its appearance will also change as a result—the skin darkens and you'll see horns and fangs appear to indicate that this is a Creature you don't want to mess with. Ultimately, your Creature will develop a set of morals which reflect the way that you play the game. You define the way you want your beast to act by punishing him when he does things you don't want him to do, and rewarding him when he does. A simple case of slap or tickle.

good vs evil

As mentioned earlier, your Creature's appearance will be determined by your actions in the gameworld. If you're ever unsure about whether your Creature is developing in the way you want him to, take note of the way he looks.

A Creature who wants to be kind and nice to the world.

A Creature who'd like to kick the world and set fire to it.

The Leashes

Successful usage of the three Leashes is a key part of the relationship that you have with your Creature. While the Leash of Learning is used to imprint actions and Miracles into your Creature's brain, the Leash of Compassion and the Leash of Aggression are also vital. No matter how your Creature has developed or the nature of his alignment (good, evil, somewhere in between?), these two Leashes can dramatically affect his attitude. Roping an evil-doing Creature to a village with the Leash of Compassion will force him to be kind to the inhabitants. Just as using the Leash of Aggression on a good Creature will urge him to be angry and destructive. Remember: a Creature's personality will also be shaped by the Leash that you use most on him.

TIP

You can place interesting things in the Pen for your Creature.

The Creature Cave

The Creature Cave in your Temple should be the one room that you visit most regularly. Here, you can not just introduce your beast to the wonders of body art, but you can keep track of his changing statistics and skills. Lionhead have included several indicators to help you monitor your Creature's development. Is he too fat to fight? Is he eating the right food? Have you taught him how to drink in order to avoid dehydration? You will find these answers on the various scrolls pinned to the wall—"Actions learnt", "Miracle Abilities", "Creature Mind" and "General Attributes". There are also three other helpful measures here: "Creature Aggression", "Creature Likes" and "Creature Miracles".

ACTIONS LEARNT

The left-hand scroll, "Actions Learnt", details the basic skills that a Creature should have picked up by the time he reaches Land Two. These talents ensure that he knows how to interact with the gameworld and its people. They are listed on this scroll as follows:

> Your Creature doesn't know how to build things.
> Your Creature doesn't know that he can take food from a field.
> Your Creature doesn't know how to use the Totem.
> Your Creature doesn't know how to use the Village Store.
> Your Creature has not learnt how to fish.
> Your Creature doesn't know how to dance.

One of your first tasks in *Black & White's* Story Mode should be to make sure that your Creature has mastered the six Creature skills mentioned. By the time you leave Land One, he should be able to take food from the fields, use the Village Store, fish and dance.

> You must learn how to care for your Creature.

Keep track of what your Creature is up to and what new things he has learnt.

You can teach him the first three by ordering him to stand near villagers who are performing the tasks. To teach him how to dance, place a rock in the centre of the village and show your Creature how people dance around it at sunset.

Learning to use the Totem and how to build new structures can only be taught on Land Two where the game's interactive tutorial continues. Leave your Creature unleashed for a while on Land Two and he should pick up any of the skills that you have missed automatically and by himself.

MIRACLE ABILITIES

Throughout the game, your Creature will attempt to learn the Miracles that you cast. You can keep track of your Creature's progress by checking the Miracle Abilities scroll. This is a lengthy list of the available Miracles and how adept your Creature is at using them. His skill in a particular Miracle is measured by a percentage score, showing just how far he has mastered its casting. When the score has reached 100 percent, your Creature has learnt the Miracle and will unleash it where appropriate—i.e. usually where he has seen you use it. Remember: some Miracles are harder to learn and cast than others. The Miracles featured in the game are all detailed in Chapter 3.

Your Creature can perform Miracles— but first, you have to teach him how.

CREATURE MIND

The Creature Mind scroll is a handy indicator of your beast's mood and attitude towards you. Here you'll find information such as "I'm a little frightened" and "My deity has paid me lots of attention". Use this scroll to balance the way that you generally treat your Creature. If you read that he is frightened, for example, try interacting with him to make him a little happier.

This scroll is a good indicator of what your Creature is thinking.

CREATURE AGGRESSION

Below three of the scrolls you'll find extra info-indicators. The Creature Aggression meter enables you to measure the attacking and defensive prowess of your Creature.

CREATURE MIRACLES

These four podiums display the Miracles that your Creature is best at and so the ones that he is likely to use most often. Use the Miracle Abilities scroll to isolate the powers that your Creature has learnt and reward him for using the ones that you want him to unleash on a regular basis. The icons for these Miracles will subsequently appear here.

You can access your Creature's attacking and defensive skills.

CREATURE LIKES

See what your Creature likes and dislikes using this indicator. The four podiums indicate what he likes to eat, attack, befriend and play with. Should a picture of a villager appear above the "likes to eat" podium, you should encourage him to snack on another food source. Villagers are, after all, a god's source of power.

The Miracles your Creature uses most often are usually the ones he's best at.

GENERAL ATTRIBUTES

Like Miracle Abilities, this final scroll is one of the more important ones. In short, by detailing the statistics below, it allows you to fine-tune your Creature's basic development. For example:

Health: Is your Creature hurt? If he hasn't learned to heal himself, you'll need to do it for him, or order him back to the Creature Pen to rest.
Alignment: Good or bad? You are his role model. A Creature's world-view will be affected by the way you play *Black & White*.
Energy: Is your Creature fit enough for the challenges ahead? Make sure that he tops up his energy levels by eating enough food.

Are you happy with your beast's attributes?

Strength: The stronger your beast, the more effective he will be in battle. Design a rock-lifting programme for any Creature who's become a 700-tonne weakling.

Fatness: The fatter your beast, the slower he'll move. It may also increase his exhaustion level. Keep him busy by sending him far across the game map and back again.

Exhaustion: A tired Creature needs rest. The most effective place to do this is in the Creature Pen.

Dehydration: Teach your Creature to drink from sources of open water so that he can automatically avoid dehydration.

Warmth: Is your Creature on fire? Well put him out! Now!

Illness: Check that your Creature is well enough to fight the good fight. Or the bad fight. Whatever your alignment.

The remaining stats are less important, providing information such as the number of animals killed and battles won. Of these, check the "Amount of Poop"—have you taught your Creature how to go to the toilet yet? Also, by keeping an eye on "Animals killed" and "People killed" you can see whether your Creature is eating properly or secretly snacking on villagers.

further creature education

Bar the six primary skills mentioned previously, what other knowledge should you be imparting to your Creature? Here are just a few pointers:

Teach your Creature to pick up villagers and put them down safely.
You obviously don't want your Creature to eat villagers as his primary source of food. Teach him that gnawing on people is wrong early on by giving him a villager. If he eats the villager, punish him accordingly. But if he puts the villager down, reward him with a tummy rub. After a couple of attempts, your Creature should learn to put a villager down if he is holding one.

Teach your Creature to drink water by clicking on the shallows.
To avoid dehydration, guide your Creature to the seashore (using the Leash of Learning) and click on the shallows to urge him to drink there. If you do this when his dehydration stat is high (see Creature Cave), he will learn to do it on his own.

TIP

Shake your hand when you've got the Leash and you'll release it.

You can teach your Creature specific tasks—such as going to the toilet!

Teach your Creature to poop by clicking near trees or rocks.

Potty training is a vital part of your Creature's development. You'll often be alerted to his need for relief by a help message; "Your Creature needs to poo". You can instruct him to go near trees or rocks by clicking near them. The Creature will also use the Creature Pen as a toilet. Did you know that you can also teach your Creature to poo in enemy villages?!

Teach your Creature what to eat.

One of the most important lessons you can teach your Creature is what he can and cannot eat. In the early days, he'll eat anything—rocks, bushes, people, even his own droppings. As usual, you can encourage and discourage his eating habits by using the "slap" and "tickle" method. Note: while grain is plentiful, your Creature will need to eat a lot of it to satisfy his hunger. Show him all food sources, including cows, sheep, pigs and horses.

Teach your Creature to sleep in the Creature Pen.

While your towering beast can kip outside under the stars, he recovers his energy much faster if he sleeps in the Creature Pen. Using the "C" button, you can monitor your Creature's tiredness. Order him back to the Creature Pen when this approaches around 85 percent. You might also want to try letting your Creature off his Leash at night.

Teach your Creature to provide Wood for the Village Store/Workshop.

Although your Creature will eventually be able to provide Wood using the Wood Miracle (see below), he can help with supplies by uprooting trees and throwing them when needed. Use the Leash of Learning when you pick up trees and dump them in the Village Store or Workshop. This way your Creature will watch your actions and learn from them, hopefully supplying Wood himself when the Desire Flags are raised.

Teach your Creature the basic Miracles.

As soon as you have access to Water, Wood, Food and Heal Miracles, you should teach them to your Creature. Ideally, you want to be able to let your Creature do most of the village-managing grunt-work—watering the fields, providing wood for the Workshop, delivering food to the Village Store. Note: you can only start to teach Miracles in the Story Mode *after* you have run the Miracles lesson.

Build up your Creature's strength and fitness.

There are several ways that you can augment your Creature's strength and decrease any extra weight he may have put on. Your Creature's Strength affects how much damage he can do in the combat arena, while how fat he is impacts on his movement. Encourage him to carry rocks over large distances by giving him a rock or using a Leash to get him to pick one up. You can also teach your Creature to play catch with rocks. Do this by throwing rocks at him until he grabs one in mid-air. Reward this action and repeat, until your beast can easily catch a rock that you throw towards him.

Your Creature will recover faster by sleeping in the Creature Pen.

Teach your Creature to convert villages.

By keeping your Creature on the Leash of Learning as you convert a neutral village, your Creature will see how you erode the Belief level in a settlement and then overturn it. Eventually, your Creature will be able to wander off on his own and convert neutral villages

Your Creature will influence a village if it's attached to the Village Centre.

before you turn your godly gaze towards them. You can manually use your Creature to influence a village by attaching him to the Village Centre with the Leash of Compassion.

Teach your Creature how to put out fires.
This is an important lesson. Not only will it be useful for your Creature to extinguish fires that start in your village, but he will be able to put himself out if attacked by a Fireball or Lightning Miracle. Combined with knowledge of the Heal Miracle, this should give your Creature a good platform for defending himself.

Teach your Creature "offensive" Miracles.
Although you can teach your Creature to throw Fireballs and cast Lightning Bolts anywhere on a game map, it is best to have him on the Leash of Learning when you attack a village held by an opposing god. In this way, your Creature will learn how to cast the Miracle by watching you do it, and will see that it should only be used on an enemy village. This hopefully avoids stray Fireballs in your own territory.

Send your Creature into battle!
You'll find that your Creature can also learn Miracles from an opponent. If you send him into battle against another god, he will be exposed to any Miracles that the opponent launches against him. This exposure will help him to see how the Miracles are cast and so allow him to gain knowledge of powers that you may not yet have access to, i.e. the Mega Blast.

creature care

Pressing the "C" button not only zooms your godly view straight to your Creature, but it allows you to quickly check on his status. This is summarised by three horizontal bars: Damage, Hunger and Tiredness. Take quick glances at this information throughout a game, so you can tell if your Creature needs a little extra help with food, healing or rest.

Training to be good

It takes very little effort to lead your Creature down a path of goodness and light. By teaching him to respect the villagers (i.e. not to eat them) and to help them out when they need resources, your Creature's attitude and alignment will change for the better. As mentioned earlier, the way that *you* play the game as a god will determine how your Creature develops. If you spend your time carefully building up your settlements, harvesting the fields and providing fish for the inhabitants, delivering trees in large quantities etc., then you'll make the people happy. If your Creature sees you do these things, he will accept that this is the way of things and try to emulate your actions.

Training to be evil

Plump for a dark and evil path and your Creature can be encouraged to destroy enemy houses, eat villagers, and strike terror into the hearts of your settlements. Again, if this is the sort of approach that you bring to the game, your Creature will attempt to mimic your actions. In both cases (good and evil), your Creature will retain the ability to provide Wood for new buildings and Water for crops in the field. Even an evil god must acknowledge that people = power.

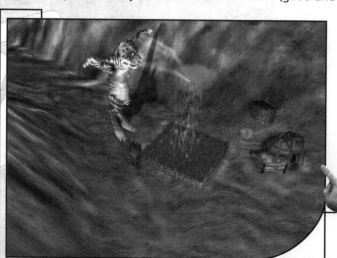

Good or evil, your Creature will always retain the ability to provide Wood and Water.

Your Creature must be able to hold his ground in a fight.

TIP

Remember: Click on your Creature during a fight and he'll defend himself.

creature combat

Although fights are few and far between in the Story Mode, you'll find that your Creature will be drawn into battle regularly in multiplayer and Skirmish games. Fights, as the manual points out, always occur in circular combat arenas and you can initiate a confrontation by leashing your Creature to another with the Leash of Aggression. Remember, however, that fights can only take place between Creatures of a similar size—no David and Goliath mismatches are allowed in *Black & White*.

While you can directly control how and where your Creature attacks, he will fight as best he can on his own. You can even zoom out from the battle arena and leave your Creature to it while you get on with some other vital godly business. Rather than demanding a fine degree of skill, Creature combat is a slug-fest—a brutal exchange of blows, Miracles and Special Moves. If you can cast any Miracles in combat (i.e. Strength, Weakness, Fireball, Heal and Lightning Bolt), then these will appear at the bottom of the screen. Each Creature also has a Special Move which, like the Fight-specific Miracles, can be cast by tracing the appropriate gestures (with no mouse buttons pressed). The Special Move can be activated by tracing the star shape. It's particularly effective in battle if you can get it right.

CHAPTER 5
Story Mode

"If it turns out that there is a god, I don't think that he's evil. But the worst that you can say about him is that basically he's an underachiever."

Woody Allen

LAND ONE

The first of the five Lands in *Black & White* functions predominantly as a game tutorial. It exists to teach and develop the key skills that you will use throughout the game—namely, movement, Creature training and basic village maintenance. Following the introductory sequence (i.e. boy meets sharks), and the construction of your temple, you're given the freedom to shape the land in your own image.

Will you be a benevolent deity (possibly with a beard), or a town-crushing, people-terrorising super-demon? Will you play through the narrative, or spend time watching your villagers chop down trees and gyrate fanatically around stone artefacts? As the game itself points out: "There is no right way to play *Black & White*." There is simply *your* way.

This section of the guide takes you through *Black & White*'s main Story Mode. Here you'll find hints on how to play the five Lands in the game and how to successfully complete the tasks triggered when you click the Gold Story scrolls. The following pages also show you where you can find the Silver Scroll challenges, how to finish them, and what magical rewards you can expect to receive for your efforts. While it's not vital for your overall progress to solve the Silver Scroll challenges, they can make playing *Black & White* a little easier. Remember, you are a god, so you should have no trouble doing several things at once...

Μαρ: Land One—Silver Scroll Challenges

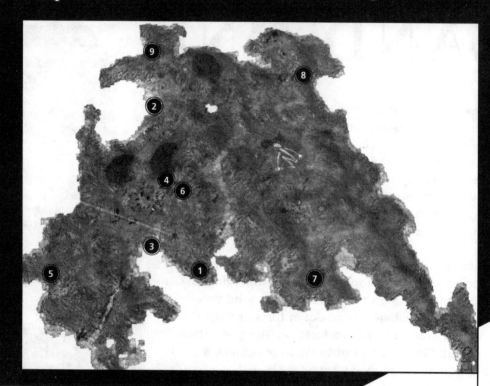

KEY: SILVER SCROLL CHALLENGES
1: Throwing Stones
2: The Explorers
3: The Saviour
4: The Lost Flock
5: The Hermit
6: The Pied Piper
7: The Singing Stones
8: The Ogre
9: The Creature Breeder*

 Note: Some challenges are only activated once you've completed certain Gold Scroll challenges.

* The Creature Breeder enables you to add extra Creatures into the game.

SILVER SCROLL CHALLENGE I
THROWING STONES
REWARDS: Beach Ball, One-shot Miracles

"Aim very carefully to hit that pillar over there. Shall we try some loosening-up exercises first?"

"Aim wildly and you might be able to hit that guy's house! Go on... Nobody's lookin'."

You'll find this challenge close to the temple, and it's one that you can quickly complete before you embark on the Choosing Your Creature challenge. The aim of the challenge is simple: use the boulders provided to knock the precariously-balanced rock off the stone pillar. You can take as much time as you like to complete the challenge—the world will still keep moving, but the story won't progress. The reward for an accurately-lobbed stone is a beach ball, and it's worth practising this rock-throwing exercise because it is also useful later on in the game. Once the challenge is complete, you can get One-shot Miracles if you knock the rock off again.

> **TIP**
> Did you know, tapping the Town Centre will exchange your worshippers with fresh ones from the town?

Instead of moving your godly hand backwards and forwards to build up momentum, simply draw it back and push it forward, letting the stone go when your hand is moving towards the target. The speed at which you perform this action determines the flight of the stone. Too much, and the rock will soar in a high arc over the pillar you're trying to hit. Too little, and it will just roll along the ground, impressing no-one. Once you have gained the beach ball, you can give it to your Creature. Teaching him to play with this prevents him from playing with more fragile things—such as villagers.

I know, let's see if we can hit that pillar over there.
Not at all. I was going to propose, er, we, um...
What do you suggest? I presume it involves killing...
OK. Let's get our projectile skills up to scratch.

Get the speed right or you'll end up looking daft.

GOLD SCROLL CHALLENGE
CHOOSE YOUR CREATURE

REWARDS: Creature (Cow, Ape or Tiger)

"All of the Creatures in *Black & White* possess an equal amount of intelligence, so it doesn't really matter which one you pick."

"Who's going to be scared of a monkey? And can you strike terror into the hearts of men with a giant cow? Choose the tiger!"

1. Although you can play around with the Norse village in this Land for as long as you like, you can only go so far without clicking the Gold Scroll in front of the big, King Kong-style gates. This activates the Choose Your Creature challenge; a vital plot chunk that encompasses three small fetch-and-carry tasks.

2. To open the massive gates, which in turn opens the way to the first Creatures, you need to find three Gate Stones. The first of these is located at the end of the ravine which you moved along after saving the boy during the intro sequence. To be honest, you can't miss it. Not only does the game's viewpoint shift to show you its location, but the Stone is helpfully illuminated with a sparkling glow. Pick it up and return it to the platform.

3. The second Gate Stone is found by clicking a scroll found near a farmhouse on the edge of the village. This activates the Lost Brother challenge, which you can complete in a number of different ways. If you're a goody-two-shoes deity, locate and return the errant villager to obtain the Stone (which is part of the nearby farmhouse). If you're developing a mean streak, use a nearby rock to smash the farmhouse so you can take the Stone without rescuing anyone. Return it to the platform.

4. To locate the final Gate Stone, activate the Sculptor challenge in the village. The Stone has been lost, but the local sculptor will carve you a new one if you can find the right type of rock. There's one in the Hermit's quarry, close to the village. Take it to the sculptor, who will shape it into the last Gate Stone. When he's finished, pick it up and put it with the other two on the platform.

Oh that's excellent. Exactly the right kind of rock to work with.

GOLD SCROLL CHALLENGE
THE CREATURE'S LEARNING (Part 1)

REWARDS: Leash of Learning, Leash of Compassion, Leash of Aggression

> **TIP**
> You can tattoo your Creature if you go to his Creature Cave and click on him.

Which do you think looks most like you?

"The way that you act in front of your Creature will not only determine how he acts, but also how he looks."

"What old beardy here is trying to say is that if you make him evil, he'll start to look a bit like me..."

The basic principles of Creature training have been lumped into a challenge called "The Creature's Learning". This is a lengthy section that covers looking after your Creature, controlling him with a Leash and interacting with objects. It's also a challenge that's split into two parts: the basic lessons are given by Sable the Creature Trainer, while the more advanced information is imparted by a giant Creature Guide.

Until you've been given the three Leashes (which marks the end of the first part of the challenge), you can't teach your Creature anything really useful. What you can do, however, is steer him towards a particular type of food. By dumping a large pile of grain in his pen, for example, you can teach your Creature to eat it. His natural inquisitiveness means that he will still try other things (cattle, trees, pigs, and so on), but by rewarding him after he has munched grain (or any other food you want him to eat), you'll start to show him that this is the food you wish him to eat. Grain is a great source of food, and one that the Creature can create himself once he's learned the Food Miracle. You'll find more information on Creature care, and the basic things you should teach your Creature in the Creature Training section of this guide.

SILVER SCROLL CHALLENGE 2
THE EXPLORERS

REWARDS: Water Miracle Dispenser

"If we aid these sailors, they'll be able to spread the word of your greatness beyond this land..."

"What'd happen if you iced a couple of the sailors? How are they gonna sail this thing without a full crew?"

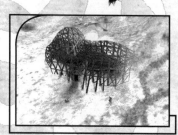

Once you've chosen your Creature, you have access to the Land beyond the giant gates—and specifically this Explorers challenge. Like the previous mini-tasks, this is a simple fetch-and-carry operation. The would-be sailors require wood and food before they can launch their boat:

1. Supply wood. You will need to supply them with around 1500 wood from your village store. They won't accept trees. Make travelling back and forth between the boat and the village easier by bookmarking the challenge site (press [CTRL] and a number—i.e. [CTRL] and the number 1).

2. Supply grain. Once the boat is finished, you'll have to plunder the village store for about 1000 food, or get it directly from the fields. Drop it next to the sailors on the beach. Note: in order to get back to the village speedily, press the [TAB] button.

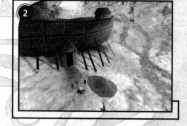

3. Supply cattle. You'll find some cows grazing close to the Norse village, near the coastline. Provide two of these for the sailors. You can also get pigs to give them as meat—they're situated next to the cows. Once you've done this, they'll launch their boat and a Water Miracle Dispenser will appear on the beach. These Explorers return later in the game.

SILVER SCROLL CHALLENGE 3
THE SAVIOUR
**REWARDS: Strength Miracle Dispenser (Good);
Anger Miracle Dispenser (Evil)**

This is a test of the fledgling relationship between you and your
Creature. In short, can you order him to pick up five drowning
villagers and then deposit them safely on the shore? Before
attempting this Silver Scroll challenge, it's a good idea to teach your
Creature that chowing down on villagers is a good-godly no-no—he
won't attempt to do this by default, but he will if you encourage him
to. Harness your beast with the Leash of Learning and click on any
villager to get your Creature to pick them up. If your Creature eats the
villager, hold the Action button and slap him repeatedly to show that
villagers aren't something that you want him to eat. Repeat this process
until your Creature can be instructed to pick up a villager and put him
back down without any toothy setbacks. Only slap him *after* he has eaten
a villager; if you slap him while he's simply holding them, he will learn not to
pick them up.

Not only is this skill useful for picking up the five people floundering in the
water here, but you'll need it for the Pied Piper challenge later on this Land.
To rescue the villagers, use the Leash of Compassion. Click on one of the
people to order the Creature to pick him up, then click again on the shore to

make your Creature carry him there and put
him down. Repeat the process four times to save all
of the villagers. Upon completion, a Strength Miracle
Dispenser is the reward for benevolent gods; an
Anger Miracle Dispenser for all you evildoers.

**These poor villagers—will
you save them, or eat them?**

**"Use your Creature to save these poor people from drowning.
You can't afford to lose any worshippers."**

**"Hey, this is a god game, not an episode
of Baywatch. I say let 'em drown."**

SILVER SCROLL CHALLENGE 4

THE LOST FLOCK
REWARDS: Pile of Food, Sheep Creature

"Let's save the farmer's lost sheep. You'll get a reward for your benevolence from the grateful villager."

"Mmm, lamb chops..."

This is a simple challenge that you can complete without the help of your Creature. Having overslept, the dozy Norse farmer has lost nine of his sheep, which are now scattered around the village in all directions. During some of the tutorial sections, you'll have spotted a few of them, and you only need to bring five back to the pen to gain your reward: a pile of food.

Return all of the lost sheep, however, and you can swap your current Creature (i.e. ape, cow or tiger) for a giant sheep Creature if you want. By doing this, your Creature's personality is transferred from its existing host into the new woollen one. The only real disadvantage is that the new sheep Creature is as small as the Creature you picked at the start of the game. If your original Creature has grown in size and strength, you lose these physical characteristics when you agree to the body-swap.

There are nine lost sheep in total. See the following pages for their locations:

Round 'em up, and get 'em penned—it's easy!

Your godly attention is required here, Leader.

map: Sheep locations 1-9

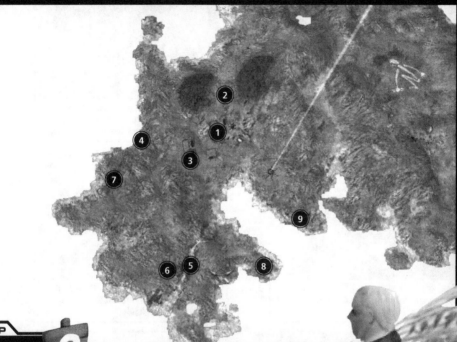

TIP

Don't just use the Temple for saving and loading—there's a wealth of info on your Creature and villagers in there as well.

You'll find a sheep next to the rocks outside the sculptor's house.

There's another lost animal just behind the giant gates on the right-hand mountainside.

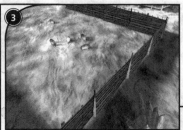

You'll find another sheep in the farm on the edge of the village, not too far from the graveyard.

Don't forget the sheep shown in this challenge's introductory sequence. It's high on the cliffs overlooking the village.

See, there's another lost sheep in the ravine where you followed the villagers at the start of the game.

Don't leave the ravine (see 5) just yet. Zoom in and you'll find another sheep clinging to the hillside.

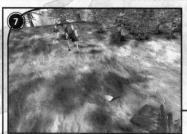

If you rescued the Lost Brother to get the second Gate Stone, you'll find another sheep in the same glade...

There's a finger of land near the ravine (see 5) where you can find a Singing Stone and another lost sheep.

You'll find the final missing sheep just behind the small hut, near the Throwing Stones challenge.

Swap your Creature's personality into the new sheep Creature by bringing your Creature to it.

CHAPTER 5: STORY MODE

SILVER SCROLL CHALLENGE 5

THE HERMIT

REWARDS: Water Miracle Dispenser, Strength Miracle One-shot

"You need to convince this lost soul that you have a Creature worthy of worship."

"Who does this guy think he is? Why don't you see how far you can throw him?"

This challenge is not necessarily one that you can complete immediately. The Hermit needs to see a Creature slightly bigger than the one you start out with—so first you have to build up your Creature's size. You can do this by getting him to carry rocks around (click on a rock to get him to pick it up) or to throw rocks (show him how to do this using the Leash of Learning). The more your Creature trains, the bigger and fitter he becomes. You'll notice the difference in your Creature's arms, as they'll become lean and muscled, while any size difference shows up when he enters or leaves his pen at the temple. You can also use the stats displayed in the Creature Cave to check on your Creature's progress.

Once your Creature is sufficiently taller, you can return to the Hermit. If suitably impressed by your Creature's largeness, he will reward you with a Water Miracle Dispenser, and point you towards a rock in the nearby quarry that hides a Strength Miracle One-shot. The Hermit will also tell you that fireflies sometimes turn into Miracle One-shots if you can find them during the day. Fireflies only come out at night, so to find out where they hide during daylight you'll need to follow them as dawn breaks and note the rocks they disappear under.

The Hermit is not easy to please, but it's worth a try!

GOLD SCROLL CHALLENGE
THE CREATURE'S LEARNING (Part 2)

REWARDS: Food Miracles, Combat knowledge

You've still got so much to learn...

Part two of "The Creature's Learning" is conducted by a giant Creature Guide and activated by clicking on the Gold Scroll behind the temple when you have completed part one. During the next sessions, you're led through the valleys towards the Aztec city, where the Creature Guide explains basic Miracle use; how to teach your Creature to cast Miracles, how to teach him to cast Miracles using One-shot Miracles, and how to impress a village. Once you've been shown how to use the Leash of Learning to teach Miracles to your Creature, set about teaching him the spells that you have found in the Land. These will include Food (Aztec village) and Water (Explorers challenge).

After a short break (encouraging you to try some Silver Scroll challenges), the Creature Guide then reveals the basics of Creature combat. This is the penultimate Gold Scroll before the one that leads to the end of the level. So, after you've learned how to fight Creature-style, you should try to complete the remaining Silver Scroll challenges before you activate the final plot sequence. It's also worth noting that this first Land doesn't teach you everything. You will discover more about Miracles and how to expand towns that believe in you on the second Land. To learn more about Creature combat and the different Miracles that you can cast, see the dedicated sections in this guide.

TIP

If you click on your Creature during a fight, he'll defend himself.

"A good god should rule firmly but fairly. Your worshippers should be taught to love and respect you."

"Don't listen to this sheet-wearing do-gooder. You need to rule through fear, terror and random acts of senseless violence..."

SILVER SCROLL CHALLENGE 6

THE PIED PIPER

REWARDS: Heal Miracle Dispenser (Good);
Lightning Dispenser (Evil)

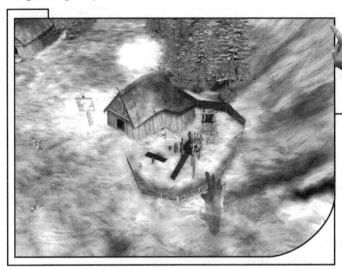

> Does your Creature have a taste for villagers?

Although this is a straightforward challenge, it can be easy to fail—especially if your Creature gobbles down the Pied Piper before you can stop him. So, unless you are happy to pursue a dark and evil path, it's a good idea to drum the following fact into your Creature's head: *DON'T EAT THE VILLAGERS*. Refer to the Saviour challenge earlier in this section for tips on how to make sure that your Creature doesn't develop a taste for villager-snacking.

> "I believe that children are our future, treat them well and let them lead the way..."

To complete this challenge, you need to capture the Pied Piper and return with him to his mountain hideaway (which lies above the village Creche). The Piper makes regular trips down the mountain, so once you've spotted him, you must attack the Leash to him (with the Creature attached to the other end)—if you fail to do this, he'll run away from the Creature. Before your Creature has time to bite off the man's legs, zoom out and click on an area just in front of the wooden doors set into the cliffside above the village. Sparing the man (being good) earns you a Heal Dispenser. Killing him without freeing the children (being evil), earns you a Lightning Dispenser. If your Creature eats the Piper it still ends the challenge and is not necessarily a failure.

> "There's probably a very good explanation for why some guy in a hood is running off with those children..."

SILVER SCROLL CHALLENGE 7
THE SINGING STONES

REWARDS: Food Miracle Dispenser

"Five Stones are missing from one of Land One's sacred circles. Each plays a different note when you tap it..."

"Hey, big guy! You're an omnipotent malevolence, not a detective agency! Haven't you got something better to do?"

"Please give me wood for my boat...", "Please find my lost brother in the forest..." It's a wonder the villagers here ever do anything for themselves. The Singing Stones challenge is another such plea. First, the Land's very own hippie sets you the task of finding five musical Stones that have gone missing from an ancient circle. Once found, you need to arrange them in order so that they play an ascending scale.

The Stones themselves are scattered across the landscape. When you find one, tap it using the Action button to see if it plays a clear note. You need to check because there are some Stones that, while they look like Singing Stones, give off a dull, almost hollow sound. Leave these where you find them and pursue only those Stones highlighted on the map on the next page:

Ever wanted to go to a Stones concert?

мαρ: **Singing Stone locations 1-5**

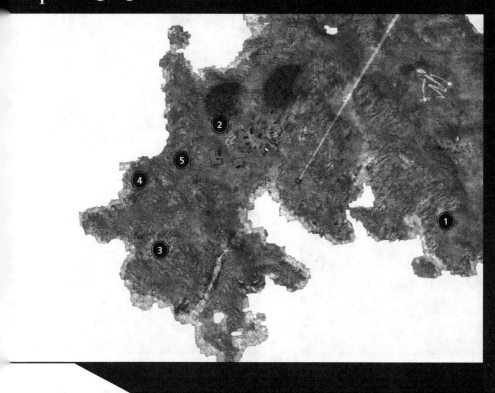

on't miss
his first one!
ou'll find it
ear the
ircle itself,
estled
gainst a
liffside.

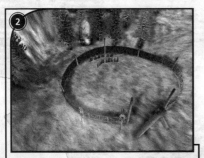

Soar back to the Norse village and you'll be able to find another Singing Stone behind the graveyard.

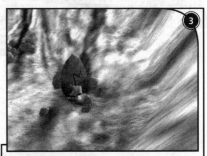

Head for the Hermit's quarry (where you found the rock for the third Gate Stone) and you'll see another Singing Stone.

Remember the wooded glade where you found the Lost Brother? There is another Singing Stone hidden away in the trees there...

Not far away from the Norse village, a river winds up a steep hillside. At the top, you'll find the last Singing Stone.

Return all of the Singing Stones to the circle and arrange them in the correct order to win a Food Miracle Dispenser.

SILVER SCROLL CHALLENGE 8
THE OGRE
REWARDS: Beach Ball, Heal Miracle Increase Dispenser

"This Ogre seems to be hiding something. Perhaps if we ask nicely, he'll let us in on the secret..."

"Now this is my kind of Creature—ugly, lazy and with no personal hygiene. I bet he fights as dirty as he smells."

Far across the island, this Silver Scroll challenge lies just outside your influence. Nevertheless, you can operate outside of your realm for a short period of time, more than enough to solve this task quickly. Like many events in *Black & White*, you can play the Ogre challenge in two ways. While the Ogre (called Sleg) skulks outside your influence, you can send your Creature to fight him. Beat Sleg in combat and you can pass through to earn your reward.

However, there is a much easier way to complete this challenge: Listen to what your conscience tells you and you'll learn that Sleg is hungry. To remedy this, soar over to your village store and pick up a good handful of grain. Fly back to Sleg and drop the food down in front of him. An animated sequence then shows Sleg eating the grain and falling asleep, enabling you to pass through to collect the goodies beyond. Although the obvious reward for your quick-thinking is a beach ball, a Heal Miracle Dispenser will also have appeared next to your temple.

Sleg in way. Sleg big ugly. Me name God...

GOLD SCROLL CHALLENGE
THE CREATURE'S LEARNING (Part 3)

REWARDS: Knowledge of Creeds, Vortex to Land Two

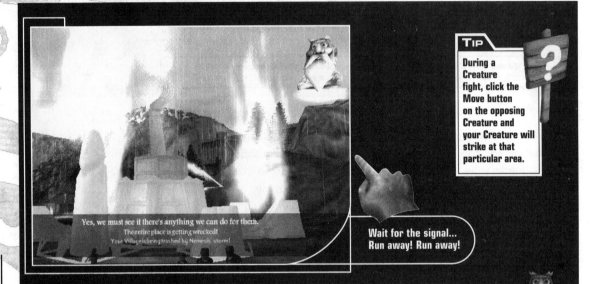

Yes, we must see if there's anything we can do for them.
The entire place is getting wrecked!
Your Village is being trashed by Nemesis' storm!

> **TIP**
>
> During a Creature fight, click the Move button on the opposing Creature and your Creature will strike at that particular area.

Wait for the signal...
Run away! Run away!

"We can't stay here forever. We have gods to confront and a universe to save from the forces of darkness."

"We ain't going nowhere. I've calculated that we need about 30,000 trees to knock together a monster sun lounger..."

Clicking on the final Gold Scroll (after the combat training), kickstarts a sequence that ends in your departure from Land One. Needless to say, if you've missed any Silver Scroll challenges or want to practise anything further, don't click the scroll just yet. By clicking on it, your Creature Guide takes you to the top of the highest mountain in Land One to tell you about the Creed. In the Lands that follow, you must find the three different parts of the Creed—they are your only defence against the self-styled super-deity, Nemesis.

During this information-dump, Nemesis himself attacks the Creature Guide with lightning bolts. Run away when you are told to by the Guide and retreat back to the village. Once the Guide has been toasted, Nemesis turns his attention to smiting the village. There's little you can do to stop him, but practise putting out fires and healing the villagers using Water and Heal Miracles.

After a few minutes, a Vortex opens to Land Two. Send through all the food and wood from your village store, plus cows and villagers (and anything else you want) before clicking on the scroll above the vortex to jump through. This ensures that you have more than enough resources to get you started in the next Land.

LAND TWO

Land Two continues your godly education, testing the skills that you've already been taught, while adding an array of new ones. Unlike Land One, where you had the luxury of manipulating a well-developed village, here you have to help your displaced followers to build one. Fortunately, you can rely on some ethereal handouts from Khazar, a local divinity who provides you with the means to erect a Temple, Village Centre, Village Store and your first house (sleeps five). In return, he expects you to help him fight rival super-being Lethys, a crony of Nemesis who you fled Land One to escape.

Your first task is to complete the construction of your core buildings. In addition to the four Scaffolds Khazar has provided for this purpose, he also gifts you a trio of Water, Wood and Food Miracles—your basic raw materials. Your Creature should already have learnt the Food, Heal and Water Miracles from Land One, so use this opportunity to teach him the Wood Miracle with the Leash of Learning. Left alone, your followers will automatically divide themselves into farmers, fisherman, foresters and builders. Slowly, the basic village structure will start to take shape, but there are several things that you can do to speed the process along.

Village expansion and maintenance is examined in detail in Chapter 2 of this guide, but for quick reference, here are a few key points to consider relevant to Land Two.

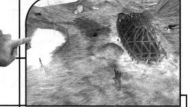

You're going to have to start showing Lethys who's boss.

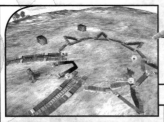

Land Two quickly introduces new concepts—be prepared.

- Lethys starts at the opposite end of this landscape. Until you have expanded your influence closer to his own
(shown in green), he will not treat you as a threat. Expect trouble, however, when you claim your fourth village.
- You are quickly introduced to the concept of the Workshop and Scaffolds on Land Two. But you cannot use them until your first village is built and you have clicked the Gold Story Scroll that explains about Worship Sites.
- Speed up the construction of your village by making five or more Builder disciples. You'll need them to build houses for your followers if you play the Workshop Silver Scroll challenge.
- Replant trees next to the Village Store so that they are easily accessible for your people. The further a Forester has to walk, the more tired he/she will become. Note: by relocating trees next to fields, you can efficiently water both at the same time.
- See the next town? Leash your Creature to the Village Centre and leave him to impress its villagers while you work to build your powerbase. To speed up the process, pick up and drop two of your villagers near the town's Village Store to designate them as Missionaries. These will spread the word of your greatness as you work elsewhere and speed up the conversion.
- One of the most important things to realise is that you can interact with the landscape in Khazar's influence as well as your own. Thus, you can plunder supplies (including new Scaffolds) so you can speed up the construction of your own village. You can even borrow people from Khazar to repopulate flagging villages. Don't worry about leaving him vulnerable to Lethys—he's a bit-player and you're interested in the much bigger plot.

ᴍᴀᴩ: Land Two—Silver Scroll Challenges

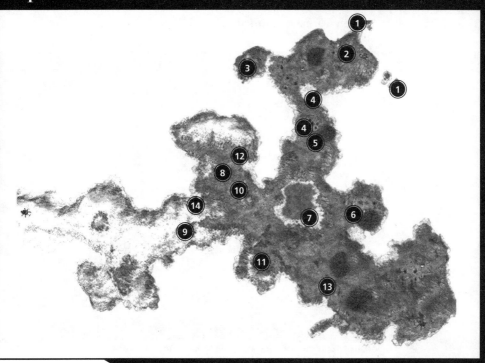

KEY: SILVER SCROLL CHALLENGES

1: Khazar's Fireball &
   Shield Challenges
2: The Workshop
3: The Idol
4: The Sea
5: The Plague
6: The Riddles
7: The Beach Temple Puzzle

8: The Sacrifice
9: The Greedy Farmer
10: The Singing Stones 2
11: The Spiritual Healer
12: The Tree Puzzle
13: The Slavers
14: The Creature Breeder 2*

 Note: Some challenges are only activated once you have completed certain Gold
Scroll challenges.

* The Creature Breeder enables you to add extra Creatures into the game.

GOLD SCROLL CHALLENGE
WORSHIP SITES
REWARDS: Prayer Power, Miracles, Workshop

building 4 completed: 31%

TIP

Worshippers get hungry and tired. Lower the Totem at the Village Centre to relieve them of their worshipping duties.

This is the first of two Gold Scrolls based on Miracle training.

"A Worship Site provides you with vital Prayer Power, which charges the Miracles you can perform."

"Bow down before me and pray, humans! I am your god! Er, I mean, we are your god... No, you are their god... Is that the time? I must be going..."

Like Land One, Land Two blends a learn-as-you-go tutorial with its empire-building gameplay—in short, it's the place where you get to put your godly skills into practice. Once the core buildings have been completed in your fledgling village, the Gold Scroll near the temple activates the Worship Sites challenge. You can't get any further in the game without it and it's the first of two Gold Scrolls based around Miracle training.

Once clicked, Khazar proceeds to explain the importance of Worship Sites and (by clicking on another Scroll near the Village Centre) how you use the Totem. Just as this friendly god provided Scaffolds for your buildings, he gifts you a Builder disciple who sets to work constructing your new Temple extension. Only when this is built (providing you with Food, Wood and Water Miracles) can you start to learn about Gestures, an equally vital Gold Scroll challenge. Completion of the Worship Sites challenge also unlocks the first set of Silver Scroll challenges; Khazar's Fireball challenge and Khazar's Shield challenge. Khazar, whose generosity seems to know no bounds, will finally provide an extra Scaffold from which you can erect a Workshop.

SILVER SCROLL CHALLENGE I
KHAZAR'S FIREBALL & SHIELD CHALLENGES
REWARDS: Fireball Miracle, Physical Shield Miracle

> "Fire can be a powerful weapon in the hands of a god who knows how to use it effectively. Practice makes perfect."

> "Look... You cast it, you aim, it, you throw it. How hard can it be? In my opinion, you can't beat a beautifully-cast shield."

After the Worship Sites challenge (and while you wait for the Workshop to be built), clicking on the Scroll near the Temple activates Khazar's Fireball and Shield challenges. Note: before you activate the Fireball challenge (located on the island with three huts), pick up and replant the trees that you find there. When the challenge begins, you'll be throwing orbs of flame at this tiny isle. Why waste the wood?

Like the Throwing Stones challenge on Land One, mastering the Fireball challenge involves getting a feel for the game's realistic physics. The flight of tossed fireballs is determined by how much power you put into the backswing. Too little and the fireball will skitter harmlessly over the ground to fizzle out in the sea. Too much oomph, however, and your red-hot bomb will miss the island and the target huts altogether.

Fortunately, you have several chances to hit the buildings that Khazar has specified. But ultimately it doesn't matter whether you succeed or fail in this challenge—the Fireball Miracle will be added to your magical arsenal regardless.

You must learn to get a feel for the game's physics.

SILVER SCROLL CHALLENGE I
KHAZAR'S FIREBALL & SHIELD CHALLENGES (Continued)

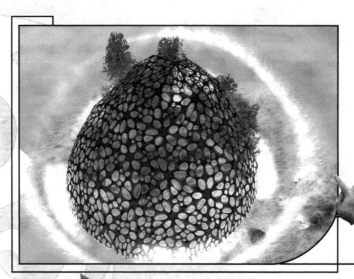

You must protect the hut with a shield.

Khazar's Shield challenge is even simpler than the Fireball challenge—you show up, you draw a circle on the ground, you get a free Miracle. It's part of the ongoing tutorial, showing you how to protect buildings with a temporary Physical Shield. First, Khazar kindly shows you how to cast and place the Miracle, before inviting you to launch stones at it to demonstrate its strength.

You are subsequently provided with three Physical Shield Miracles and challenged to protect the hut shown here with a shield of your own. The trick is to trace a circle around the hut that is slightly bigger than you actually need. This ensures that the resulting shield is big enough to fully shelter the target building underneath its magical dome. Note that Physical Shields can be breached if they become heavily damaged, and that the amount of damage is determined by the size of the object that you throw at it. Like the Fireball Miracle, the Physical Shield Miracle is then added to your available powers. Your powers grow accordingly.

SILVER SCROLL CHALLENGE 2

THE WORKSHOP

REWARDS: Forest Miracle

> "It's really important that you construct enough buildings to shelter your young disciples."

The Workshop is a straightforward challenge, but one that can significantly strengthen your position on Land Two. In *Black & White*, gods are only as powerful as the number of people that believe in them, and so your villagers should be regarded as your most precious resource. For a population to thrive and expand, the people need houses to live in—the more space that you give them, the more they have the opportunity to fill it.

By holding your godly hand over the Village Centre, you can quickly see what the current population is and how many houses you need to build. In addition to the large hall already built

> "Houses? Waste of time and resources if you ask me, boss. Focus instead on expanding your evil influence."

(which sleeps five villagers), you should aim to construct three large Abodes. You can cheat slightly by relocating some of your villagers to the next town to reduce your own population and therefore the number of houses required. If this second Norse settlement hasn't yet been converted, you can designate a few Missionary disciples to kickstart the process. There are some conveniently empty spaces in the houses here, enabling you to complete the Workshop task a lot faster and with less environmental effort. Clicking on the Silver Scroll when the required houses are completed, wins you the extremely useful Forest Miracle.

This challenge can strengthen your position on Land Two.

GOLD SCROLL CHALLENGE
GESTURES & INFLUENCE
REWARDS: Gesture knowledge

> "You can cast any of the Miracles you know by moving your hand in the appropriate way. Trace a W to summon water..."

> "We're going to drench people to death? What are we: almighty or all-wussy?"

Use of Gestures is vital to your expansionist ambitions in *Black & White*. The ability to summon Miracles with a particular movement of your hand means that you don't have to return to your Temple or Village Centre to charge one up. This lesson, the final tutorial scroll in this landscape, shows you how to access your magical arsenal by tracing a clockwise spiral of energy on the ground. The Miracles available, and the Gestures needed to activate them, are detailed in their own section in this guide.

Once you have mastered *Black & White's* godly graffiti, Khazar then challenges you to fill the neighbouring Village Store with grain (you may have converted this town already). Deposit food in this store using either a series of Food Miracles or by harvesting nearby fields, catching fish, or transferring food from your own store. Continue until Khazar butts in to tell you that the store is now full to bursting. Khazar then shows you the next town (Indian) that he wants you to take over, so that you edge ever closer to a confrontation with Lethys. Before he leaves to defend his realm, he tells you that you can perform some Miracles and actions outside your influence. But only for a short time. Now you know enough to start building an empire in this land.

TIP

There are Miracles hidden all over Eden, so be sure to always keep your eyes peeled.

You must learn how to summon Miracles.

GOLD SCROLL CHALLENGE
GESTURES & INFLUENCE (Continued)

You must "impress" the nearby Indian village.

Once you've expanded to convert the second Norse village (located near your home settlement), your next target is the nearby Indian village. After this has been "impressed", you'll find that you can expand in one of two ways. The safer route is to head for the Indian village that lies just outside Khazar's blue spheres of influence. A tougher test of your resource-juggling skills comes if you direct your attention towards the other Indian village—the one which lies right on the fringe of the green-bordered lands ruled by Lethys. Of course, the big "L" may have conquered this one already, making it several times harder to acquire.

As more villagers equals more power, the best tactic is probably to grab the unclaimed villages first. That means sending your Creature to convert the free Indian village near Khazar and then the free Greek settlement nearby. This will give you a total of five villages, a good powerbase from which you can launch attacks against Lethys (and, if you're feeling a little evil, to double-cross Khazar). Most importantly, you'll ultimately have access to a wide range of Miracles: Wood, Food, Water, Fireball, Physical Shield, Forest, Heal, Teleport, Spiritual Shield, Strength (Creature) and Aggressive (Creature). As you progress, you'll also have the opportunity to activate a variety of other Silver Scroll challenges. Take a look...

SILVER SCROLL CHALLENGE 3
THE IDOL

REWARDS: Fireball Miracle Increase

> "Goodness me, there's a villager over there worshipping some sort of statue. We didn't build that!"

> "Hey, maybe he's sucking up to some new goddess. And maybe that goddess has a sexy lady conscience. Oh boy!"

The Idol challenge is a test of your divine morality. Appearing midway through Land Two, a rogue villager has constructed an idol of his own and is praying to it instead of praying to you. Obviously, you need to destroy the offensive icon and possibly its blasphemous creator. Good gods can attempt to reintegrate this lost soul into society; bad gods might want to launch him in a satisfyingly-high arc out over the ocean. What wins you the reward in this challenge is the destruction of the idol, not how nicely you treat the villager-turned-cultist.

As you'll quickly discover, the idol is too big for you or your Creature to move. Throwing rocks or trees at it also has little effect—you won't be able to get near it at all if you haven't converted and looked after the Norse village nearby. What *will* destroy the idol, however, is fire. The Fireball Miracle on its own is next to useless. You need to construct a bonfire around the idol by piling trees up around it. When you've amassed enough wood— the more fuel, the better—cast a Fireball Miracle directly at the pyre, or light a tree and use it as a match to ignite the others. Once lit, the idol becomes super-heated and explodes. Your reward? A more powerful Fireball Miracle.

The Idol is too big for you or your Creature to move.

SILVER SCROLL CHALLENGE 4
THE PLAGUE
REWARDS: Food, Lightning Bolt Miracle

This Silver Scroll challenge is related to your rule of the third settlement you encounter—the Indian village. While you've been learning how to build new structures and cast Miracles with a simple gesture, Lethys has been expanding fast. In short, you've got to convert the Indian village to your cause before Lethys gets his disembodied hand on it. This forms part of the Impress Village Story Scroll. You'll see another Gold Story Scroll here too. This activates the Destroy It part of the plot and explains that you must smash Lethys' temple to triumph on this second Land.

> "We need to stop this plague from spreading. Let's find the source of the sickness and treat it quickly."

The Plague challenge appears shortly after you have converted the Indian village—your evil conscience will alert you by saying; "Hey, Lethys is doing something over in that village, boss." Clicking on the scroll above the Indian tent, you'll discover that the villagers have been poisoned. You need to find the source of the dreadful poison and heal the sick—a true godly task. Float over to the Indian Village Store and you'll see that the food has become green and rancid. Get rid of the spoiled chow by picking it up and dumping it in the sea, or burning it. To complete the challenge, you only need to use the Heal Miracle that you gain from the second village. The trick here isn't to try and heal all your people, but to keep some alive and to feed everyone without using the poisoned Village Store.

> "Hey, is that food supposed to look green? In the other villages, it has a far healthier yellowy-brownish colour to it..."

Remember, you can't activate the Totem in village two (and the Heal Miracle) before that settlement's Worship Site has been constructed at the Temple.

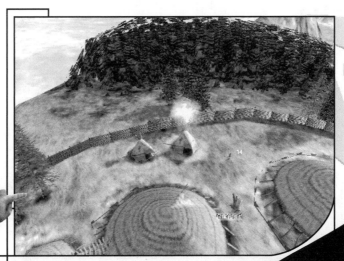

Show that Lethys that you're prepared to fight.

SILVER SCROLL CHALLENGE 5
THE SEA
REWARDS: Enlarge Creature Miracle

> "We have to look after our followers—they are the very source of our mightiness."

> "(Sings) Ohhh... I've got this notion that I'd quite like to smack your face in..."

This challenge won't appear until the Plague challenge is completed, and even then it won't be available in the first Indian village immediately. In essence, it's a much simpler version of Land One's Saviour challenge, with a similar pluck-the-villagers-from-the-water premise. This time it's a group of errant children who have got into difficulty—you can find them near the jetty at the bottom of the cliff. Because you've already converted this village, the drowning kids are well within your influence. Use your Creature to grab them from the sea and deposit them safely on the bank, whereupon they'll go running back to mummy.

When all the children have returned to the large hut in the village, you'll get a reward—a Miracle Dispenser that charges up Enlarge Creature One-shots. It may not seem as exciting as a Lightning Bolt Miracle, but the this potion can be very effective if you want to quickly gain large chunks of Belief in new settlements. Villagers tend to be more impressed if they see a Creature the size of a small mountain. Doubly so if it waters their crops, or ruthlessly kicks their Crèche in.

You've already had practice at saving people from water.

SILVER SCROLL CHALLENGE 6
THE RIDDLES
REWARDS: Zebra Creature

Found on the edge of the Indian town near Khazar's realm, the Riddles challenge asks you to find three objects, place them inside a mushroom ring, and then cast the appropriate spell on them. The ancient riddle goes thus: "Place in the ring something that howls at night, something hot, something unique to your creature, then all must be protected." So you'll need:

- A wolf
- A burning bush/tree
- A lump of your Creature's poo
- A Physical Shield Miracle

You must place the objects inside this mushroom ring.

You need to place the first three items in the ring and, making sure that they are all within the mushroom circle, cast a Physical Shield Miracle around (and over) them. By now, lumps of Creature poo shouldn't be too tricky to find—and if you can't, just guide your trusty animal to some trees or rocks and wait for nature to take its course. Use the Fireball and Physical Shield Miracles that you obtained from completing Khazar's challenges. The wolf is the only tricky ingredient to find. They're rarely around during the day, but you can pick one up around the Beach Temple lake at night. Your reward is the opportunity to swap to a new zebra Creature.

"Hmmm. What object could possibly be 'unique' to our Creature?"

"Beardy, you're talking a load of poo."

SILVER SCROLL CHALLENGE 7
THE BEACH TEMPLE PUZZLE
REWARDS: Continuous Healing Miracle

"Look, another tiny person in distress. We can play this puzzle even though it might lie outside our influence."

"Pipe down, cloud-butt! So the guy gets flooded once in a while. Boo-hoo. We've got a world to terrorise!"

There are many of these logic puzzles scattered across the five Lands in *Black & White*. In this one, you need to move a Temple from its position at the water's edge to another site further up the beach. The Temple consists of four pieces—from the smallest (the roof) to the largest (the base). We've designated them A, B, C and D respectively. Thus A is the small roof piece, B is the slightly bigger roof piece, and so on. The poles on the beach, meanwhile, have been numbered 1, 2 and 3—where 1 is the current location of the Temple and 3 is where you're challenged to move it.

You must move the Temple further up the beach.

Remember: a Temple piece can only be placed on top of a bigger piece.

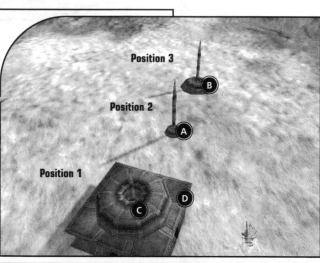

Position 3

Position 2

Position 1

TIP

Disciples are very useful—they will perform any task you assign them, till death.

You must shift the Temple using the correct sequence.

Remember: a Temple piece may only sit atop a piece that is bigger than itself. So, for example, you *cannot* put the base of the Temple (D) on top of the smallest roof section (A). By using the following sequence, you can shift the Temple from position 1 to position 3 in 15 moves.

Move A to 2
Move B to 3
Move A to 3
Move C to 2
Move A to 1
Move B to 2
Move A to 2
Move D to 3
Move A to 3
Move B to 1
Move A to 1
Move C to 3
Move A to 2
Move B to 3
Move A to 3

By completing this puzzle, you earn an everlasting Heal Miracle.

Completion of this puzzle turns the Beach Temple into a giant Heal Miracle. Anybody who visits it is immediately revitalised. A good spot for a new village, perhaps?

SILVER SCROLL CHALLENGE 8

THE SACRIFICE

REWARDS: Prayer Power boost, Heal Miracle Increase

"These people are prepared to kill their son to show their devotion to you, leader. Tell them they don't have to!"

"If the kid dies, you get a boost to your Prayer Power, boss. And you could use it right about now..."

This challenge won't appear until you have converted the Indian village that lies close to the Celtic territories ruled by Lethys. Once your Worship Site for the village is in place, a priest offers to sacrifice a child in your name. Do you fling the sobbing kid onto the altar and gain a 5,000 boost to your Prayer Power? Or free him, sacrifice something else, and gain a Heal Miracle Increase for your benevolence? Kill the priest and you may even deter others from following his example.

The Sacrifice is part challenge, part subtle game tutorial. Whatever your decision, you learn that by feeding objects to a Worship Site, you can quickly charge up any accessible Miracles. Offer up a sheep, for example, and 800 is added to your Prayer Power total, while 1,000 and 1,200 are added for a cow and horse respectively. Pop a villager onto the altar and he'll be converted into around 4,000 units of power. Even plants can be sacrificed—they have a low boost value (small shrubs typically add 100 units, large trees 500), but whoever heard of a society built upon the ritual slaughter of plantlife? Unless you're looking to create a utopian vegetarian settlement, the spilling of blood is always better than sap.

This is part challenge, part game tutorial.

SILVER SCROLL CHALLENGE 9

THE GREEDY FARMER

REWARDS: Lightning Bolt Miracle Increase

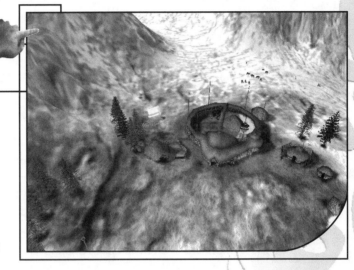

This challenge is well worth completing.

You may not have the time to complete any of the challenges as you fight your way towards Lethys, but some are well worth the trouble. Take the Greedy Farmer episode, for example. Located in the snowbound Celtic village (the one furthest away from Lethys' Temple). If you manage to solve it correctly, your attacking options will be augmented by the gift of a more powerful Lightning Bolt Miracle. Not bad for ten minutes work.

Once activated, you learn that a band of unruly children has been stealing a farmer's cattle. The children in question operate out of a small hut down by the coastline. Periodically, they run up the hillside in order to steal one of the cows that graze in the snowy area next to the Village Store. As ever, *Black & White* lets you tackle the situation in a number of ways. Kill the farmer, perhaps? Kill the thieving children (you'll have to wait around for them)? Kill all the cows so nobody can have them? Watch what happens and you'll see that the kids are pinching cows because they're starving. Provide them with a nutritional alternative and you may just win that Lightning Bolt for your kindness.

"Oh my! What is that disgusting smell? I think it's you. When did you last take a bath?"

"Do you see a tub around here, pops? Well, do ya? We live in a cranium, not a condo. Jeez..."

SILVER SCROLL CHALLENGES 10, 11 & 12

THE SINGING STONES 2
REWARDS: Dove Miracle Dispenser

You should try to play a melody on these stones.

Rather than having to find the Singing Stones (as you may have done in Land One), here you're encouraged to play a melody on them. The keeper of the stones speaks of secret tunes and "special powers" waiting to be unleashed. You must play Twinkle, Twinkle, Little Star as follows: 1, 1, 8, 8, 9, 9, 8, 6, 6, 5, 5, 3, 3, 1. Night now falls and the stones transform into gravestones. Now you must play the Funeral March as follows: 2, 2, 2, 2, 5, 4, 4, 2, 2, 1, 2.

Perform this successfully and you can place anything which has recently died, like a human body or a skeleton, into the glowing circle and it comes back to life. This ability disappears after a few minutes.

This is more of a moral dilemma than it is a challenge.

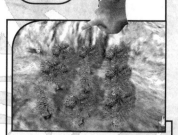

This puzzle's solution is not so easy to come by.

THE SPIRITUAL HEALER (HIDDEN CHALLENGE)
REWARDS: None

Note: This is a hidden challenge so there is no scroll to activate it. Children are being sacrificed in order to keep all the older people alive. If you remove the culprit (a good act) those who are being kept alive all die and you'll lose followers. If you allow him to remain, you get the follower numbers, but you'll have committed an evil act—it's a moral issue. A solution would be to leave him until your other villages are strong enough to withstand the death of all the undead people the healer is keeping alive. So you deliberately do an evil act for the sake of having more prayer power and more influence. You can leave this challenge running in the background if you like.

THE TREE PUZZLE
REWARDS: Dove Miracle Dispenser

Not strictly a Silver Challenge, this Puzzle is activated by clicking on the "?" signpost next to it. The basics of the puzzle are simple, but the solution is not so easy. The puzzle presents a random arrangement of trees every time you play. All you need to remember is that when you pick up a tree, it changes the species of those trees adjacent to it (as long as they are on a horizontal or vertical line). A Dove Miracle Dispenser is ample reward for any tree-uprooting persistence.

SILVER SCROLL CHALLENGE 13
THE SLAVERS
REWARDS: Extra villagers and worshippers

"I'm sure that there's a completely non-violent way to defuse this situation and free the frightened villagers from slavery."

"Nah, we've got to teach these scumbags a lesson that they'll never forget. Cry havoc and let loose the giant hand!"

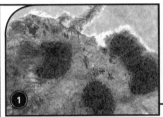

1. Find the lions here.

Some of the villagers are missing, and it seems that the slavers up yonder hill are holding them captive. These flesh-traffickers challenge you to capture wild beasts for a circus they want to start. In return, they'll free their slaves—on a beast-per-slave basis, naturally. You can either undertake the task that the slavers set for you (see below), or murder all the traders and free the slaves yourself. Doing this solves the challenge, but doesn't get you any manpower. So the goody-two-shoes, non-violent way really is the right one, freeing the slaves and gaining you extra worshippers as a bonus. Wanna play? Then find the following animals and place them in the circular pen near the slaver's temple.

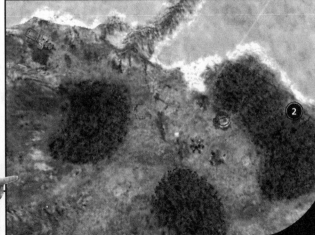

2. You can find the wolves in this area.

SILVER SCROLL CHALLENGE 13
THE SLAVERS (continued)

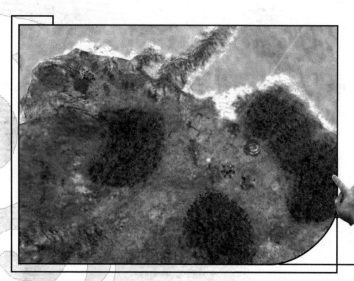

3. You can find the horses in this area.

1. 2 x Mountain Lions—you can find these animals wandering on a nearby hillside. For every lion you supply, the slavers will free two villagers. They won't accept more than two, though.

2. 1 x Wolf—pick up one of these cunning hunters (worth two slaves) near the village in which this challenge is set. You'll find a pack of them sunning themselves near the sea behind the Village Store.

3. 2 x Horses—hardly the most exotic beasts, but every good circus needs a couple of nags. Find these grazing nearby or outside the first Indian village you converted. Supply a pair to free two slaves.

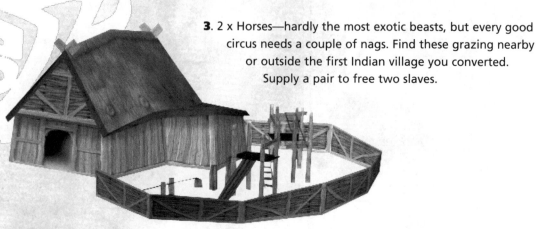

GOLD SCROLL CHALLENGE
KHAZAR DIES, LETHYS FLEES
REWARDS: Vortex to Land Three

"I don't believe it. The mighty Khazar
has been completely obliterated. Perhaps
we should seek a truce with Lethys?"

"Truce? No way! We live in a god-eat-god world.
Anyway, that Lethys ain't so tough. We can take him."

In addition to the Silver challenges detailed on the previous
pages, there are two other significant events that shape
the narrative on Land Two. The first of these is the death
of your ally, Khazar. Once you've taken four villages, you
can only watch as Nemesis suddenly opens a vortex from his
own realm (Land Five) to rain fiery hell onto Khazar's home village.
During the onslaught, Khazar's Temple and his Creature are destroyed. You discover that
Khazar's Creature held a part of the Creed inside him—but this is stolen by Lethys. Khazar's
lands are now free to be converted by both you and Lethys, so spread your religion quickly.

Your aim, as ever, is to invade, impress and convert your godly way towards Lethys. When
his last village falls, and you're finally in a position to strike at his Temple, the final plot
sequence kicks in. Again, you're but a helpless bystander as Lethys abducts your Creature
and transports him through a vortex into Land Three.
When you regain control, click on the Gold scroll
rotating above the vortex to follow.

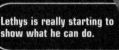

Lethys is really starting to
show what he can do.

Follow your Creature through
the vortex to Land Three.

LAND THREE

rriving in a new Land brings with it a new set of problems, the biggest being that you'll have to play the majority of Land Three without your Creature's help. For now, your Creature stands frozen between three pillars, a prison constructed by Lethys and maintained by the Prayer Power of worshipping villages. As ever, you start this Land at the opposite end of the island from your target. But your aim remains the same—expand towards Lethys by impressing and converting the villages you come across en route. This time, however, one of the pillars holding your Creature disappears every time you win a new settlement.

Again, you have to start building your home village from scratch. Fortunately, Scaffolds for the construction of your Temple, Village Store, Workshop and Village Centre have already been provided and, left to their own devices, your villagers will slowly build them. The first problem you face is a shortage of food (few fields) and wood (palm trees). Note that the trees next to the temple grow faster than palm trees, so they provide more wood as they get bigger. The rocky landscape here also means that your core buildings are rather inconveniently spread out. Note, however, that you have the best supply of rocks on the entire landscape. They'll come in handy later.

Village expansion and maintenance is
examined in detail elsewhere in this
guide, but for quick reference, here are a
few key points to consider that are
particularly relevant to Land Three.

You have to play most of Land
Three without the help of your
ever faithful Creature.

You'll need to impress
this village nearby.

- Provide all the wood for your core structures and set Builder disciples to work to
  speed up construction. Note that once your Temple and Village Centre are complete,
  and the Worship site is erected, you'll have instant access to Fireball, Heal, Food,
  Storm, Water and Wood Miracles. Without your Creature, you'll need all the power
  you can get.
- Your village's fields are very spread out on this land, so designate a couple of Farmers
  to keep the Food rolling in.
- Once the Workshop is finished, your villagers will start constructing a Crèche and extra
  houses on their own. This leaves you free to concentrate on impressing the Japanese
  village in the valley below. Remember: by expanding your influence, you also expand
  your borders, making it much more difficult for Lethys to attack your powerbase.
- Harsh weather conditions may lead to the odd lightning strike. To combat any
  damage, make sure that you assign villagers to the Worship Site as soon as it's ready.
  This will give you access to the Water Miracle, and will help you put out any fires that
  flare up.
- When you get into a position to start impressing the Japanese village, the first (and
  most important) Silver Scroll appears nearby. This gives you access to the Shaolin
  challenge and will eventually unlock information about tribal Wonders. Admittedly,
  this challenge can be frustrating to complete, but it's worth it and makes playing Land
  Three that much friendlier.

ᴍᴀᴘ: Land Three—Silver Scroll Challenges

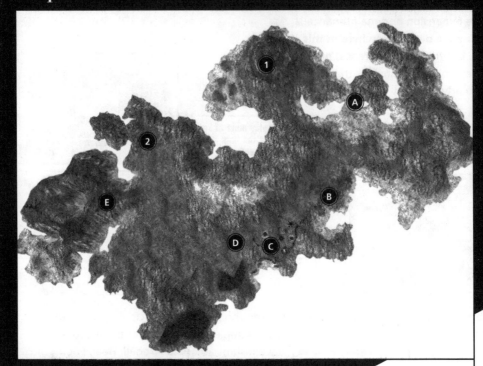

KEY: SILVER SCROLL CHALLENGES

1: The Shaolin
2: The Rejuvenator

KEY: EVENTS

A: Throw Bloke
B: Fire! Fire! I'm on Fire!
C: The Wolves Are Possessed
D: The Shaolin's Wonder
E: Creature held captive

 Note: Some challenges are only activated once you have completed certain main or Gold Scroll challenges.

THE FIRST VILLAGE

REWARDS: Activation of Shaolin challenge

Converting the Japanese village in the valley below adds Lightning Bolt and Teleport Miracles, plus Physical and Spiritual Shields, to your existing arsenal. But talking about claiming this town is one thing; actually doing it is another. Your sphere of influence here isn't big enough to let you reach out and drop a Missionary in the village. Consequently, you need to find an alternative way of showing off in front of the inhabitants. From a distance, all you can really do is hurl objects in their general direction. Rocks and small but surprisingly aerodynamic shrubs will gain you around 10 Belief units per projectile. But it'll still take you a long time to overturn the 500 unit total doing this.

Obviously, you need to expand your influence so that you're within striking distance of the target village. When the Workshop is finished, create a single Scaffold and build a little two-man hut on the pathway leading down to the Japanese settlement. Place the Scaffold at the very edge of your influence—thereby expanding your shimmering red border. From here, you should be able to place a couple of Missionaries near the closest houses and cast a couple of Miracles to go with them. If you find that you still can't quite reach the village, build another tiny hut to extend your influence further. Once you start to impress the Japanese village, the Shaolin challenge appears.

"Every time we convert a village, one of the statues holding our trapped Creature will simply disappear."

TIP
Simply tap on joined Scaffolds to dismantle them when necessary.

"Hey, this first village is too far away. But we can throw stuff at it to impress the people there... Hand me a big rock."

You must think of ways to expand your influence.

SILVER SCROLL CHALLENGE I
THE SHAOLIN

REWARDS: Help with the Fanatic Attack and the Wolf Attack challenges, Knowledge of Wonders

"This guru values his solitude. Let's respect his privacy and leave him alone. We've got to rescue our Creature."

"Don't listen to beardy, boss. This weirdo is hiding something. We gotta find out what it is."

Your mission, should you decide to accept it, is to tail the Shaolin to his secret place of worship. Once he has begun his stroll down the mountainside, slowly follow him by grabbing the landscape and by tapping the "Z" button to rotate the view. It's vitally important that you: (a) stay behind the Shaolin, and (b) keep him in view at all times. Failure to do either of these things will result in the cessation of the challenge and you'll be forced to start again. Initially, it's not too complicated, and you can easily shadow the Shaolin through the rocks and the trees. After a short while, he'll stop and a sparkle appears on the ground. Think of this as a "Save" point. Should you be spotted after this, the challenge will be restarted here instead of back at the Temple.

The Shaolin now continues his journey, moving from the first "Save" point towards a cluster of blue mushrooms. When he enters this fungal circle, he will turn to look out over the cliff. If you're still behind him at this point, you'll be spotted—challenge failed. To stay hidden, rotate your godly view (using the "U" key), so that you remain behind his back as he turns. He'll pause here for a while, then turn around to continue his journey. Use the "Z" key to rotate the view behind him again and move on.

The next obstacle you face is when the pathway disappears underneath a huge boulder. If you lose sight of the Shaolin

Stay behind the Shaolin and keep him in your view.

You must find the Shaolin's secret place.

as he walks under this rock, you will have to reactivate the challenge and start all over again from the last "Save" point. To make things easier, press "P" to pause the game, and zoom in the view so that you are close behind the Shaolin at almost ground level. Adjust the pitch to keep your target in view, then restart. As the Shaolin walks through, he'll veer off to the right (as you view from behind). You should not lose sight of him, because you can effectively look through the rock. After this, another sparkly patch of ground indicates another "Save" point.

There's another mushroom cluster next. Deal with it in the same way as you did the first one—i.e. rotate the view behind him as he turns to look out over the landscape. After this, you'll approach some red mushrooms and another rock-over-the-pathway obstacle. Again, zoom in and make sure that you keep the Shaolin in sight at all times.

Following this, the oblivious guru will walk to the cliff-edge to look out over the landscape again. But if you stay behind him, he won't be able to see you. The Shaolin's secret place lies up ahead: a flat rock between two pillars. When he reaches here, he promises to help you later in this Land. You have now completed the challenge.

EVENTS

FIRE! FIRE! I'M ON FIRE!
REWARDS: None

> "Lethys has set fire to some of our worshippers and they're coming this way! Put them out before they reach the village."

> "Why waste your Prayer Power, big guy? Just pick them up and chuck them into the sea. No fussin'."

Impress and convert the first village the best way you know how. A miraculous Food Miracle here, a Wood Miracle there. Vary your strategies to get the maximum amount of Belief from the village's inhabitants. Throwing a villager about in front of a crowd seems to work wonders. Sure it's a process of attrition, but eventually you'll wear them down.

When you manage to take the village under your divine wing, Lethys will make a dramatic appearance, scoffing: "You still dare to oppose me?!" The evil god then cruelly sets fire to a group of your new villagers who then run wildly in your direction. If you have previously completed the Shaolin Silver challenge, the badly-dressed guru will appear and provide two One-shot Water Miracles to help you drench your fiery friends. These won't get you far, though, so you'll still need to rely on the Water Miracle from your Temple. If you haven't done

Lethys demonstrates his cruel nature by setting fire to some of your villagers.

Do your best to keep your village from being torched.

the Shaolin challenge, use your Water Miracles the best you can. The worse-case scenario is that you haven't completed the Shaolin challenge and haven't got enough Prayer Power to charge Water Miracles quickly. If this is the case, throw the burning citizens into the sea so they don't torch the village.

EVENTS

THE WOLVES ARE POSSESSED
REWARDS: None

"We should take time to strengthen our hold on the villages we have, holy one. Expand too fast and we'll be vulnerable."

"Are you nuts? If we don't get to the second village before the big L does, it'll be tougher to take over. Hey! Are those wolves?"

> **TIP**
>
> Fires can spread very quickly—you must deal with them before it's too late!

Taking the first village puts you within striking distance of the second one. Ideally, you need to impress and convert this village before Lethys gets his hands on it. Again, perform an array of impressive Miracles and gestures: throw trees around, lift people up and put them on top of houses—you know the drill by now. Unfortunately, as you race for this settlement, so does Lethys. With Lightning Bolt, Forest, Water and Fireball Miracles to be gained, it's strategically important for both of you.

If Lethys captures the village before you can reach or convert it fully, you face an uphill battle for control. Should this happen, you can divert the other god's attention by lobbing rocks at the third village in the distance. Cause enough damage and it should give you the breathing space to start eroding the Belief Lethys has amassed in village two. If, at any point, Lethys returns to reinstate his rule, attack his other village again to keep him out of the way. There are more detailed hints and tips for capturing an enemy-held village in the relevant section of this guide. When you've finally gained control here, another one of the pillars trapping your Creature will disappear. Unfortunately, Lethys is so angry at this point that he sends in another attack.

As an encore to the flaming fanatics who tried to singe your first village, Lethys now sends a pack of hungry wolves towards your second settlement. Again, if you have already played the Shaolin challenge, the guru kindly appears and destroys most of the rampaging beasts. Prevent the remainder from snacking on your villagers by picking them up and hurling them across the landscape. They shouldn't survive the flight. If you didn't play the Shaolin challenge, however, you have to deal with all the wolves yourself. The same grab-'n'-hurl tactics apply, but the task is much harder.

Attack Lethys' villages to keep him out of your way.

TIP
Experiment with different ways of throwing people and objects.

Defeat the wolves and you'll have some time to consolidate your position and to strengthen the villages that you control. For now, the third village (whose inhabitants maintain the last pillar holding your Creature) is too far away to be effectively influenced. Make sure that you have enough resources to keep your population thriving. Wood is plentiful in the middle of the island, but the availability of Food can be a problem. There are no huge fish stocks to speak of, so you might want to expand your production capacity by adding to the fields that you already have. Convert any animals you find into Food too. You want to be well-prepared, and well-stocked for the battles to come.

EVENTS

THE SHAOLIN'S WONDER
REWARDS: Knowledge of Wonders, Wonder

"Did I say leave the guru alone? Did I really? Well, um, your mightiness, I might have got that wrong."

"Boss, that's why you should always listen to me. Dump the goody-goody attitude. Let's get evil."

Spend some time maintaining your villages and the Shaolin will announce that he is giving you the ability to construct a Wonder. This new building helps increase the range of your influence and augment your power. It requires around 10,000 Wood, but once erected gives your village's birth rate an enormous boost—with different Wonders affecting different aspects of the game. More importantly, this super-folly provides a vital stepping stone to the village that's powering the final pillar keeping your Creature on ice.

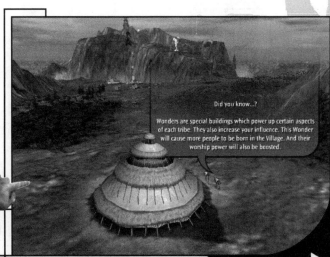

Did you know...?

Wonders are special buildings which power up certain aspects of each tribe. They also increase your influence. This Wonder will cause more people to be born in the Village. And their worship power will also be boosted.

Wonders provide your people with increased happiness and a larger zone of Influence.

Because you're building the Wonder close to Lethys' territory, you may want to protect the building site with a Physical Shield Miracle. But once the Wonder is completed, you're ready to attack that final village—just be prepared for a long slog. Held stubbornly by your enemy, around 1,500-worth of Belief in Lethys needs to be overturned before this settlement will fall under your control. And without your Creature's help it can be a long process—casting Miracle after Miracle, providing extra resources, throwing trees, people, rocks and so on. Remember: you can play both the good and the bad guy when trying to impress a village. Don't hesitate to unleash a Lightning Bolt to torch a few houses, then help put out the fires with a follow-up Water Miracle.

"At last, our great Creature's free! Now we can return to our full and—dare I say it?—frightening strength."

"Hello, is that Oblivion? I'd like to book a one-way ticket for my buddy Lethys. Worst class seat, please..."

EVENTS
LETHYS
REWARDS: Vortex to Land Four

When the third village falls under your influence, your Creature is finally free. Press "C" to zoom in on him and check for damage—he'll probably need to recuperate before you can use his talents effectively. However, there's still much to do. Your hold on the third village needs strengthening and the worshippers constituting the core of your power need looking after. But don't kill them through over-worship. Note also

Once you've secured the third village, your Creature will be free.

that another Silver Scroll challenge, the Rejuvenator, has appeared nearby. To complete Land Three, you now need to try and convert Lethys' last village, located in the hills near his Temple. Naturally, Lethys won't take kindly to your interference—particularly since this remaining settlement is now the only source of Belief he has left, and if he loses it, he'll cease to exist. Of course, Lethys will do all that he can to keep hold of this last bastion of faith, so you should expect to go one-on-one with his Creature. Defeat it and you give yourself some breathing space to make an impact on his village. When he's significantly threatened by your actions, however, and the Belief levels in his settlement start to plummet, Lethys will offer his surrender. In return for sparing his life, he immediately opens a vortex to Land Four. Note: if you choose to destroy Lethys, you'll find that the Land Four vortex is hidden underneath his Temple.

TIP

If you place a tree in your village, it will become a scenic addition and will please your people. Foresters will not cut them down.

SILVER SCROLL CHALLENGE 2

THE REJUVENATOR

**REWARDS: Fountain Of Youth,
Ape Creature**

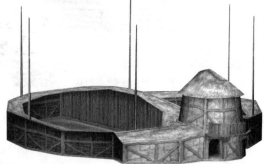

Not so much a challenge, more of an opportunity, this one. The Rejuvenator offers what amounts to a fountain of youth: the ability to reduce the Age statistic of those villagers who are clamouring for free Teleport passes for the over 65s. Take a 70-year-old hag to the Rejuvenator, for example, and she'll work her magic to make the septuagenarian into a four-year-old kid. Rather than encouraging your villages to have more children, why not stem the death rate and keep everybody eternally young?

Of course, by the time you can access the Rejuvenator, you'll be well on the way to beating Lethys on this land. So sending all of your villagers for an age-related makeover hardly seems worth it. There is, however, another side to the woman's powers. Send her a young villager and she'll accidentally turn them into a new Creature—an Ape or a Chimp. Like a typical Creature Breeder (which you'll be familiar with from the earlier Lands), simply bring your existing Creature to the hut and click on the Creature that you wish to swap to. Your Creature's personality and powers are then copied from one to the other. If you don't warm to your new acquisition, you always have the opportunity to change back.

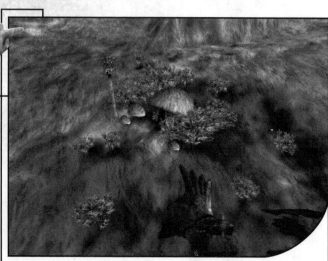

A great opportunity to give the old folk a youthful glow.

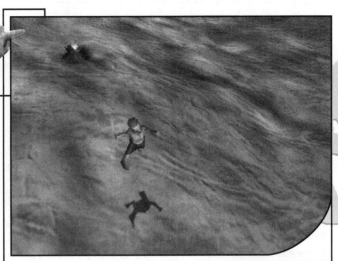

This bloke seems to have a few godly powers of his own.

TIP

Throwing villagers around is great fun—but some seem more durable than others!

EVENTS
THROW BLOKE
REWARDS: None

Pressing the "S" key near the Shaolin's mountain should direct you to a man sitting on the beach below. Although he looks like any other *Black & White* villager, this lonely soul is impossible to kill. There's no real reward for trying to kill him, but you can have fun throwing the poor guy across the game map. Throw him into the sea and he won't drown. Set fire to him and he won't incinerate. Hurl him at a mountainside and he'll merely complain about a bump on his head. Amazing!

"Man or indeed woman should not meddle with the forces of nature. No good will come of it."

"No 'good'? The Rejuvenator said she can roll back the years and get rid of my flabby man-breasts. I'm sold!"

LAND FOUR

his fourth level returns you to Land One, which is now a dark, fire-ravaged wasteland—while some of the original buildings remain, they're all half-built or damaged. The first decision you face is whether to rebuild the shattered village infrastructure or take time out to look around. But with deadly lightning randomly stabbing the landscape and fireballs raining down on the poor village inhabitants, there's a chance that any good work you do will be instantly undone by Nemesis' magical ire.

Ideally, you should provide enough Wood for the completion of your core village buildings. Haul fish from the sea and dump them in the centre of the settlement, then set Farmer disciples and Builders to work the available fields. The aim is to provide your people with just enough resources so that they can exist while you pursue this land's three-part quest. You must protect your town from fireballs as some do damage, some don't. Use a Shield Miracle and build the town up between fireball attacks. To save Land Four, you need to find and destroy three Guardian Stones. One is held under a Physical Shield near an unclaimed village, another is protected by a giant Ogre backed by a legion of Gremlins. The last one has apparently been given to a devout worshipper of Nemesis, who lives alone atop a hill far away from your starting point.

Village expansion and maintenance is examined in detail in Chapter 2 of this guide, but for quick reference, here are a few key points to consider that are relevant to Land Four.

Your people will still need you to provide for them...

...so don't get too preoccupied with your search for the Stones....

- It's important to provide your villagers with everything they need to stay alive while you roam the landscape in search of the Guardian Stones. Their wellbeing is directly linked to your own power—provide enough Wood to complete the basic buildings, especially the Temple and the Worship Site that comes with it.
- Once the village Workshop is completed, you need a Village Store (cost: three Scaffolds).
- Pause the game ("P") and scout around. Locate and bookmark the three Guardian Stone locations as shown in the Land Four intro sequence, so that you can soar quickly towards them. These have been designated: The Bell Puzzle, The Defending Ogres and The Heartbroken Man. They are explained in detail on the pages that follow.
- Note the other main points of interest on this land. There's a small, unclaimed village near the Guardian Stone protected by the Physical Shield—this needs to be converted before you can access The Bell Puzzle. Further inland, a circle of huts (without a Village Centre) nestles in a large crater, while a third village is built on a hilltop on the opposite end of the island (see Map on following page). You'll eventually need to convert the available villages, especially if you want to complete all of the Silver Scroll challenges that this Land has to offer.
- Once you've provided sufficient resources for your villagers to start the rebuilding process, you need to choose which Guardian Stone to pursue first. Beating The Defending Ogres causes the lightning to stop, while solving The Bell Puzzle calls off the bombardment of fireballs. Completing the The Heartbroken Man finally returns the sky and the landscape to normality.

TIP

Water your fields to improve crop yields; a Water Miracle does the job nicely.

nd Four—Silver Scroll Challenges

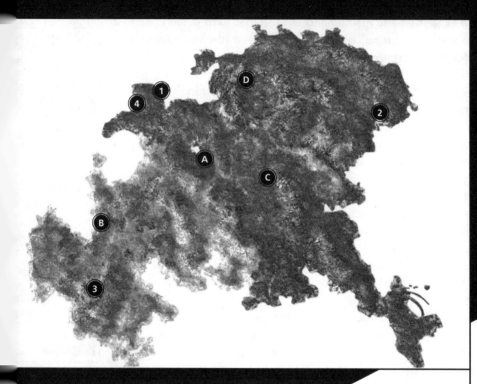

KEY: SILVER CHALLENGES

1: The Fish Puzzle
2: The Blind Woman
3: The Thesius Puzzle
4: The Creature Breeder*

KEY: EVENTS

A: The Bell Puzzle
B: The Defending Ogres
C: The Heartbroken Man
D: The Undead Village

 Note: Some challenges are only activated once you've completed certain Gold Scroll challenges.

* The Creature Breeder enables you to add extra Creatures into the game.

TIP

Attacking Village Centres and Village Stores brings villagers back from the Worship site.

GUARDIAN STONE I
THE DEFENDING OGRES
REWARDS: Guardian Stone

Faced with a choice of starting either The Bell Puzzle or The Defending Ogres mini-quest, we suggest that you choose the latter. Why? Well, if you leave the Ogre on this land alone for too long, his tiny minions (the Gremlins) periodically raid your fragile village and carry off the inhabitants. With lightning strikes and fireballs to deal with, this is an extra problem that your villagers could do without. To start The Defending Ogres, locate the Ogre in his hideout on the coast and order your Creature to go there.

"That terrible smell, those ugly looks... Surely that creature can't be the same Ogre that we met before?"

Yeah, what was his name? Slug? Or was it Slag? And who are those little guys following him around? What an ugly bunch!"

The Ogre guarding the Guardian Stone is Sleg, son of Sleg. In this mini-quest, there's no puzzle to solve or fetch-and-carry task to complete. Instead, you must face the ugly giant in the combat arena, a one-on-one face-off between Sleg and your faithful Creature. This showdown will auto-start once your Creature gets close enough to Sleg's beach-front home. It's a fairly straightforward slap-fest, and providing that your Creature is big enough and strong enough to hold his own, you should have no trouble defeating Sleg—see the Combat section earlier in this guide. Victory gains you the Guardian Stone and causes the rain and lightning to stop (at least over your village).

Make sure your Creature has what it takes to beat this ugly beast.

GUARDIAN STONE 2

THE BELL PUZZLE

REWARDS: Guardian Stone

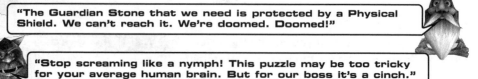

"The Guardian Stone that we need is protected by a Physical Shield. We can't reach it. We're doomed. Doomed!"

"Stop screaming like a nymph! This puzzle may be too tricky for your average human brain. But for our boss it's a cinch."

Before the Scroll appears that lets you begin The Bell Puzzle (and to dispel the Physical Shield protecting the Guardian Stone), you need to bring the nearby village under your godly rule. By now, your Creature should be an old hand at village conversion and it shouldn't take too long to erode the 500 Belief needed to win it. The very sight of him, plus a few well-timed Miracles, should be all that you need. You can speed up the process, by lobbing trees at the settlement from the hilltop above—people are always impressed by the sight of flying timber. Once the village accepts you as its latest omnipotence, a Silver Scroll appears next to The Bell Puzzle.

In essence, The Bell Puzzle is *Black & White's* own version of Simon Says. To dispel the Shield here, you need to repeat the tunes played on the five white bell towers. Click on the Silver Scroll to activate the challenge.

The Bell Puzzle consists of five bells mounted atop five white stone towers. There are four rounds of Simon Says that need to be completed, and in each round you must play

Concentrate hard on remembering the correct order of the bells—you don't have much time in which to play them back.

back the bells in the order that they are played to you. Note that you only have a short time to play each of the bells in sequence—hesitate too long and you'll fail the challenge. Also, you don't actually need to click on the bell itself; you can get away with just clicking the towers that hold them (which is much easier). Finally, make the process even simpler by using the "Z" key to rotate the default view, so that you can easily see and touch all five towers at the touch of a button.

Using the Action button, click the towers/bells in the following order (looking from left to right along the line).

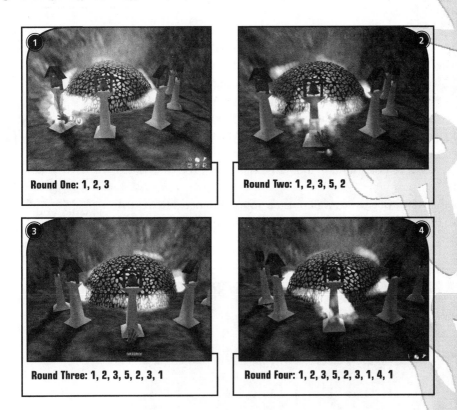

Round One: 1, 2, 3

Round Two: 1, 2, 3, 5, 2

Round Three: 1, 2, 3, 5, 2, 3, 1

Round Four: 1, 2, 3, 5, 2, 3, 1, 4, 1

If completed successfully, the Physical Shield is dispelled via five white-hot bolts of light. The Guardian Stone is then destroyed and a part of Nemesis is vapourised. Thankfully, the part in question seems to be the bit that's been throwing the fireballs at your home village, because now these stop bombarding the landscape. Two stones down, one to go.

GUARDIAN STONE 3
THE HEARTBROKEN MAN
REWARDS: Guardian Stone

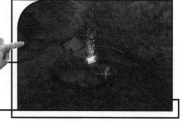

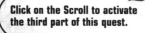

Click on the Scroll to activate
the third part of this quest.

"We should reunite this poor man with his lost wife. The power of love is a force that cannot be denied."

The third part of the Guardian Stone quest is activated by clicking on a Scroll which appears after you've solved The Bell Puzzle and defeated the Ogre. You'll find it over a small farmhouse in the middle of the island (shown here) and not far from the Nemesis-worshipping loner who lives high on the hill. The woman who lives here explains that her reclusive neighbour, Adam, is being forced to worship Nemesis because his wife Keiko has been forcibly taken from him. Fortunately, the woman knows that Keiko can be found in the Aztec village not too far away.

As the Aztec village lies well outside your influence (see below), you'll need to convert it before you can go any further.

"I haven't got jiggy with a lady in over 4,000 years. But then you probably don't even know what 'jiggy' means."

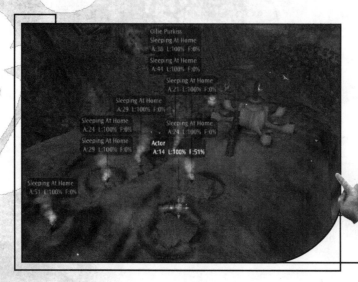

Now you'll need to convert the Aztec village.

Adam's tent is, unfortunately, outside of your influence.

You will have to find a way to get Keiko home to him.

The Aztec village may lie far away from your Temple and the basic sphere of influence that it gives you, but you can complete this challenge using your Creature. Assuming he's well-trained, fit and healthy, send him over to the Aztec settlement to impress the villagers. Tying him to the Village Centre with the Leash of Compassion (and restricting his movement) usually does the trick. Once the 500 Belief deficit has been overturned, press the "S" key to locate Keiko (she should be identifiable as an "Actor").

Because Adam's tent lies outside of your influence, even with the conversion of the Aztec village, you'll need to instruct your Creature to carry Keiko home. Order him to pick her up in the village and then set his destination to a point just outside Adam's abode. When you accomplish this fetch-and-carry task, the third and final Guardian Stone is destroyed and the land returns to its former blue-green glory. Note: you can also pick up and kill the woman, which accomplishes the same end. You must then trigger the Undead Village scroll to locate and reveal the Creed Element.

Before you finish the level, why not try and complete some of the Silver Scroll challenges and Puzzles that this fourth land has to offer? See the following pages...

THE THESIUS PUZZLES

REWARDS: Creature Strength Miracle Dispenser

"Guide the boy away from the wolf to earn a reward that may help you conquer this harsh landscape."

"No, no! Guide the kid *towards* the wolf. Oops, he's dead. Do it again, and again. The carnage never ends!"

These maze puzzles (there are two to negotiate in Land Four) are simple to understand, yet can be difficult to complete. The aim in both is the same—guide the boy Thomas out of the labyrinth while avoiding the hungry wolf. The boy can only move one square at a time, after which the wolf takes a move. As a rule, the wolf always moves towards the boy, unless it finds its way blocked by an obstacle.

The solutions here require that you view the Thesius maze with the "?" signpost at the bottom of the screen (as shown). The starting points, and the route you should take to

escape the mazes, have been marked. Note that you can attempt the puzzles as many times as you like, while the game world continues to function in the background. Successfully complete both of the Thesius puzzles here (the second is activated upon completion of the first) and you're rewarded with a Strength Miracle for use with your Creature.

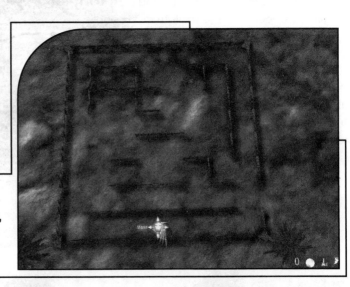

Not so hard to understand, but a little harder to complete.

Thesius Puzzle 1.

Key

Boy Start	●
Wolf Start	■

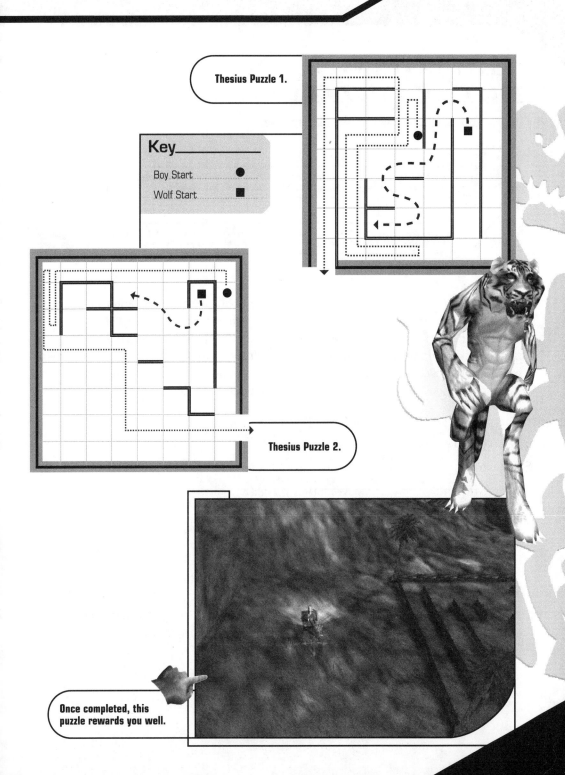

Thesius Puzzle 2.

Once completed, this puzzle rewards you well.

THE JAPANESE TOTEM PUZZLE

REWARDS: Spiritual Shield Miracle Dispenser

"By solving these puzzles, we can gain extra Miracles to help us in our fight against the powers of evil."

"Or by solving these puzzles we can gain extra Miracles to help us be more evil. It cuts both ways, Boss."

This logic puzzle is another distraction from your godly tasks on Land Four, a non-essential, brain-stretching extra. It shouldn't be confused with the main Bell Puzzle, which forms part of this Land's narrative. Located on a hill near the coast, this puzzle features six Totems which you must pull up and raise to their full height. The movement of one Totem typically affects the height of one or more of the others. Viewed from the "?" signpost, pulling one Totem moves its neighbours as follows:

Totem 1	Moves Totems 2 and 6
Totem 2	Does not affect other Totems
Totem 3	Moves Totems 1, 2 and 4
Totem 4	Moves Totem 3
Totem 5	Moves Totem 6
Totem 6	Moves Totems 4 and 2

A Totem sparkles at the base when it's extended to its full height. The reward for successfully completing this puzzle is a Spiritual Shield Miracle Dispenser.

SILVER SCROLL CHALLENGE I
THE FISH PUZZLE
REWARDS: Turtle Creature

TIP
Fish Farms can provide food for your village. A Fisherman will deliver his catch to the Village Store when it's big enough.

This is a simple puzzle which requires good hand-eye coordination. By now you should be aware that tapping the water near fish scares them something rotten.

In The Fish Puzzle, you need to use this skill to guide the shoal of fish into the net for the young Fisherman. The best tactic here is to herd the two separate shoals into one large one, which is easier to control with a bit of divine intervention.

The reward for your persistence in this puzzle is the ability to change your current Creature for a Turtle. A Silver Scroll now appears above the new Creature—click on it when your own Creature is nearby to perform the swap.

"As the land is safer now, let's help the inhabitants rebuild their shattered lives. Like this Fisherman here..."

"Oh yeah, now this one is going to look great on our resumé: all-seeing, all-knowing, all-powerful (but will fish for cash)."

SILVER SCROLL CHALLENGE 2

THE BLIND WOMAN

REWARDS: Water Miracle Dispenser

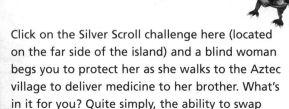

"Look, leader, a Silver Scroll! Another chance to impress the people with our goodness and kindness."

"Don't you ever get sick of all this grovelling? I say we evict Goodie and get a new head-mate. How about it?"

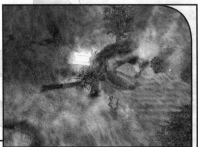

Click on the Silver Scroll, complete the challenge, and you'll be rewarded with the opportunity to get yourself a new Creature.

Click on the Silver Scroll challenge here (located on the far side of the island) and a blind woman begs you to protect her as she walks to the Aztec village to deliver medicine to her brother. What's in it for you? Quite simply, the ability to swap your current Creature for a Wolf.

Interested? All you have to do is watch over the woman as she travels, helping her negotiate three perilous obstacles. For starters, use *Black & White*'s Bookmarking facility to tag the woman—she's much easier to see with a big, yellow "7" floating above her head, so you won't lose sight of her against the gloomy landscape. Now you'll encounter the following terrors:

1. Wolves—these lurk in the first ravine that you encounter. Scout ahead until you locate them, then simply pick them up and throw the ravenous beasts out of the way. Alternatively, if you have any offensive spells powered, use these to remove the canine threat. If the wolves attack the woman you're supposed to be protecting, you'll have to start the challenge again.

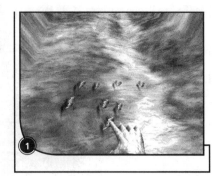

2. Forest Fire—after you've dispatched the wolves, a fire breaks out in the trees up ahead. There are several ways you can deal with this: activate Water or Storm Miracles to put the flames out, or remove the trees from the woman's path by hand. However you do it, make sure the inferno is extinguished before your charge gets close.

3. The last obstacle is a grumpy Ogre who has been unable to sleep because of the constant bleating of sheep. Either heal the woman or swiftly remove the offending animals from the hillside nearby, so that your charge can walk safely by the monster. Be quick about it or the Ogre will attack her and you'll fail the challenge.

4. Guide the woman past all three obstacles (you get three chances to do so), and she will reach the Aztec village and heal her brother. As a thankyou present, the brother now offers you the chance to swap your current Creature for a Wolf.

TIP

Bookmarks can be set on any person or object capable of some kind of movement.

GOLD SCROLL CHALLENGE
THE UNDEAD VILLAGE
REWARDS: Part of the Creed, Vortex to Land Five

> "We're nearing the end of our long journey in this land, leader. We are almost ready to take on the evil Nemesis."

> "So he turned an entire village into undead zombie skeletons... So what? It's not a curse, it's a tourist attraction."

Once you've destroyed the three Guardian Stones and loosened Nemesis' grip on Land Four, a Gold Scroll challenge appears in the village near the five bell towers. Click on it and a man appears to tell you the story of The Undead Village. Located in a large crater outside your Influence (see map earlier in the guide), this village is little more than a small circle of huts. It seems that Nemesis cursed the village, burying the two Totems that provided them with their power and transforming them into animated skeletons. Your task is to lift the curse—only by doing this will you find part of the Creed and open the vortex to the final Land.

You need to complete this challenge in several stages:

1. Your ultimate aim is to restore the village's Totems to their original positions. To do this, you need Influence, so you can operate freely in and around the crater, and this means constructing a new Village Centre there.

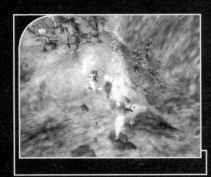

GOLD SCROLL CHALLENGE
THE UNDEAD VILLAGE (Continued)

2. Combining five Scaffolds together gives you the ability to construct a new Village Centre. Use the fact that you can operate outside your Influence for a short time to place the Scaffold as close to the Undead Village as you possibly can. Transfer a villager from your home settlement and designate him/her as a Builder disciple to start work on the new structure. Note that if you have placed the Scaffold close enough to the Undead Village, the skeleton inhabitants will help you erect the Village Centre themselves. If not, you'll need to place down another Village Centre—preferably right in the middle of the village.

3. Speed up the construction of the new Village Centre by bringing in more Builder disciples and providing more Wood and Food for the task in hand. If the Village Centre has been placed close enough, the skeletal citizens adopt it as their own and you'll find that there's the usual 500 Belief total to be overturned.

If you have built it too far away, the Village Centre automatically falls under your control, maintained by the Belief of the Builders who constructed it. If your extended influence doesn't encompass the two Totems on the crater's edge, you need to build another Village Centre closer to the huts.

GOLD SCROLL CHALLENGE
THE UNDEAD VILLAGE (Continued)

TIP
If your Creature picks up rocks, it makes him stronger.

4. Once you've converted the Undead Village, you'll have a sphere of Influence that enables you to interact with the buried Totems. There are two of these, and you have to raise both to break the curse on the village. While you can easily pull the Totems out of the ground, they slowly sink back down again afterwards. It's impossible for one god to keep both of them raised without a little help.

5. The solution lies with your Creature. Summon him to the crater and make him watch as you raise and lower one of the Totems. Repeat this process several times, using the Leash of Learning to drum the lesson into his animal brain. With practice, your Creature will learn how to raise the Totem by himself. When he proudly demonstrates his newly acquired skill, use your hand to lift the other Totem so that both are standing. When both are fully-raised, the curse on the village is broken and the elated villagers will tell you the location of the Creed part you seek—it lies atop the highest hill, inside the skeletal remains of the Creature Guide.

GOLD SCROLL CHALLENGE
THE UNDEAD VILLAGE (Continued)

6. Even if you've converted all of the available villages on Land Four, the mountain where Nemesis blasted the Creature Guide still lies outside your Influence. Only your Creature can reach and retrieve the Creed part for you. But when he does so, Nemesis opens a vortex to his world (Land Five) and invites you to come through for the final battle.

6

17

Creature Guide

7. With the vortex open, you have the opportunity to send through provisions and villagers to get you started on the other side. Remember: you can send almost anything through the vortex—Miracle seeds, animals, piles of Wood and Food, trees and even rocks. You don't have to send anything through (there will be enough basic resources in Land Five to get you started), but it's

7

worth giving yourself the best chance of survival possible. Land Five is, after all, Nemesis' own backyard. Click on the Scroll above the howling vortex to jump through. The end game approaches.

LAND FIVE

With Khazar and Lethys defeated, only you and Nemesis remain to fight for control of Eden. As you'd expect, Land Five is dominated by your opponent, and Nemesis has made sure that your corner of this Land is far from impressive. Not only are the basic resources (i.e. Wood and Food) scarce, but before you can do anything, an invisible force curses your Creature. The malady is twofold, reversing the alignment of your Creature and slowly draining him of power. This will obviously affect his effectiveness.

As usual, you need to establish your home village quickly—you don't want to be without your miraculous powers for long. To get close to Nemesis, you'll need to methodically convert the villages that he controls. Naturally, Nemesis will fight you every step of the way, and you'll find that you need to employ all of your skills and knowledge to expand your influence and keep the gains you make. Attack one village, while trying to convert another. Seek out the Silver Scroll challenges to add extra powers to your arsenal. You'll probably need to build a Wonder to give an extra boost to your powers and resources. Which will work best: a Blitzkrieg-style expansion or a slow, deliberate build-up? Questions, questions. You need answers, answers.

Village expansion and maintenance is examined in detail in the dedicated sections of this guide (Chapter 2), but for quick reference, here are a few key points to consider that are relevant to Land Five:

Your resources are scarce and your Creature is losing power. You must act fast.

- As mentioned previously, there are few trees to be found around your starting point. Make good use of the ones available nearby to build your Temple and Worship Site first. Set disciples to work in the fields near the half-built Workshop and haul fish from the sea to satisfy your villagers.
- If you completed the Explorers challenge back on Land One, you'll get an extra, fully-formed village with a clickable Silver Scroll and (possibly) its own small Norse Wonder. If you missed this challenge, all you'll see are empty fields. But note the shoal of fish swimming in the sea nearby. There is another Thesius maze puzzle nearby which gives you the chance to swap your current Creature for a Lion, arguably the king of *Black & White's* bestiary.
- A mysterious Miracle Dispenser lies hidden underneath some heavy rocks on the mountain near your Temple. This Dispenser glows at night making it easier to find. The Dispenser allows you access to a Fireball power-up level 1. There is one village on Land Five that hasn't yet fallen completely under the control of Nemesis. This is the Tibetan village which will eventually give you access to powered-up Fireball, Lightning Bolt, and Heal Miracles, plus Teleport, Forest and Megablast. Although this village will be protected by a Spiritual Shield when you try to convert it, once taken, it will allow you to play the Magic Dragon Silver Scroll challenge nearby.

TIP

If you click the Action button on any house, you can see how many people live in each house in the entire village.

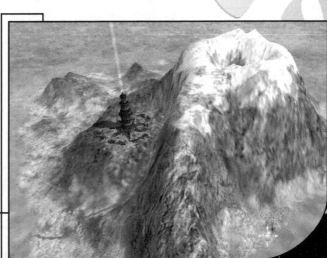

The mountains on this Land accommodate more than just snow!

map: Land Five—Silver Scroll Challenges

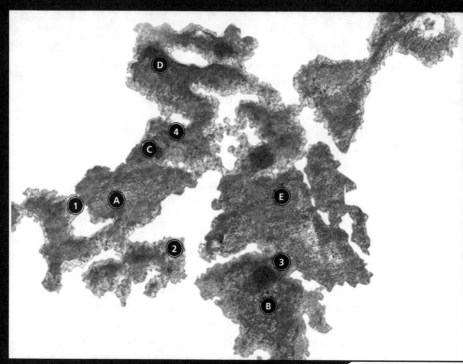

KEY: SILVER CHALLENGES

1: The Explorers Again
2: The Lion Puzzle
3: The Magic Dragon
4: Swap to Brown Bear

KEY: EVENTS/FEATURES

A: Fireball Miracle Dispenser
B: Tibetan Village (with Shield)
C: The Japanese Helper
D: Nemesis Wonder (saps Creature's strength)
E: Nemesis Wonder (reverses Creature's alignment)

Note: Some challenges are only activated once you've completed certain main or Gold Scroll challenges.

SILVER SCROLL CHALLENGE I
THE EXPLORERS AGAIN
REWARDS: Extra Village, Polar Bear Creature

If you helped the Explorers build their boat way back on Land One, you'll find that they have reappeared on a stretch of land close to your own starting area. Your reward is twofold. First, you'll have gained control of a fully-formed village—very handy considering that your own home settlement starts as a series of building sites. Not only is this bonus village well-developed (look, a Crèche!), it adds extra people to your fledgling empire. As you know by now, more people ultimately means more power. Better still, this new village should also feature a Norse Wonder on the hill above it.

TIP

Silver Scrolls are not vital—you don't have to do them. However, the rewards are often worth the effort.

"On Land One, demon, you said that we shouldn't have helped these explorers. Now they're back to help us."

"They didn't choose this place. It chose them. These guys didn't moor their boat, they crashed it! They ain't going anywhere now!"

Look closer and you'll find a Silver Scroll hidden in the remains of the boat you helped them to build. Click on it and you'll be given the option to swap your current creature for a polar bear. The basic characteristics of this rare animal are detailed in the Creature Comforts chapter. Is there a tricky quest to complete before you can do this? A fetch-and-carry task to perform? No, you simply click on the Silver Scroll to get the reward. The Explorers didn't really show any gratitude for your godly efforts on the first Land. Giving you the Polar Bear is their way of saying "thanks".

You'll be given the opportunity to swap your Creature for a polar bear.

SILVER SCROLL CHALLENGE 2
THE LION PUZZLE
REWARDS: Lion Creature

"By solving the puzzles scattered around the landscape, we gain rewards such as Miracles or new Creatures."

"With respect boss, do we really have time? Our Creature is already big and strong. Although not as nasty as he could be..."

Similar to the Thesius puzzles on Land Four, in this single puzzle you need to guide the hungry lion to his sheep dinner. To make things difficult, both lion and sheep are in a maze. To make things doubly tricky, the lion is blind and will walk in the direction you point him until he can't move forward any further. This solution assumes that you are viewing the maze with the "?" signpost at the bottom of the screen. If you aren't viewing it this way, do so now. The starting points, and the route you should take to solve the puzzle are marked. Successfully complete the Lion puzzle and you will be rewarded with the chance to swap your current Creature for a Lion.

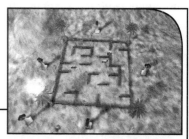

This puzzle is well worth solving—you'll get the chance to swap to a lion Creature.

TIP

Press F1 when your hand is over an object and any information concerning that object will be displayed.

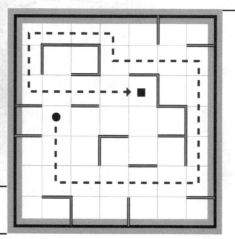

Key

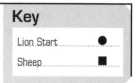

Lion Start	●
Sheep	■

The Lion puzzle.

CHAPTER 5: STORY MODE

THE TIBETAN VILLAGE

REWARDS: Extra Village, Access to Silver Dragon challenge.

From a distance, the Tibetan village here looks like an easy target, but the only way you can begin to gain Belief there is to send your Creature. As your giant animal approaches, however, Nemesis will spot the threat and raise a Spiritual Shield over the settlement. This is no ordinary dome of protection either—the Shield is powered by three stones, each amplifying the Prayer Power of a villager. Until the Shield is dispelled, you can't hope to make an impression on the villagers.

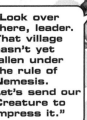

"Look over there, leader. That village hasn't yet fallen under the rule of Nemesis. Let's send our Creature to impress it."

"I don't know, boss. Our Creature has been acting a little cuckoo lately. I say we tie him up and beat some sense into him."

To solve this mini-puzzle, direct your Creature (using the Leash of Compassion) to one of the stones until he is close to the villager dancing around it. Click on the cavorting citizen with the Action button to urge your Creature to pick him up. Once he has done this, the villager's concentration is broken and the link he had with the stone is severed. Repeat this process for the remaining two stones and the Shield will eventually fall. This will leave you free to influence the town and to incorporate it into your empire. You can access the Magic Dragon Silver challenge without converting this village. But you'll need the Influence that conversion supplies to access the challenge's reward.

Your Creature needs to be close enough to pick up this dancing villager.

Focus Creature

189

SILVER SCROLL CHALLENGE 3
THE MAGIC DRAGON
REWARDS: Winged Creatures Miracle Dispenser

"(Sings) Puff the Magic Dragon, lived by the sea, he frolicked in the Autumn mist, in a land called Honnolee..."

"Do you actually understand what that song is about? I mean do you really? It's not about a talking lizard you know..."

Although you might be able to access the Magic Dragon challenge without converting the Tibetan village above, you won't be able to complete it. Clicking on the Silver Scroll here introduces you to a group of crusaders who are preparing to battle a dragon. The giant, fire-breathing lizard in question is hiding out in a cavern and the crusaders have a cunning plan to defeat it. They will only tell you of this plan, however, if you heal them all back to full health. Only when your home village is functional and its Worship Site is built will you have access to the Heal Miracle they need.

When you do finally manage to treat them, they tell you that their plan is to fill the dragon's cavern with smoke (so it won't be able to see), then to rush in and kill it. Unfortunately, they don't have the means to light the pyre that they've built to provide the all-important smoke. The Fireball Miracle is also available via your home settlement. Once the pyre is ignited, the crusaders charge in. Click on the Silver Scroll again to get further instructions. Follow the crusaders by listening at the craters until they finally appear out of a doorway on the opposite side of the hill. High on adrenaline, they offer

you a Winged Creatures Miracle Dispenser which they've found inside.

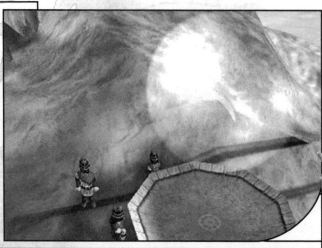

Heal the crusaders and they'll repay you with valuable information.

GOLD SCROLL CHALLENGE
THE JAPANESE HELPER
REWARDS: Swap To Bear Silver Challenge

"I'm sure that if we all sat down around a table together, we could find a way to live alongside Nemesis in peace..."

"Is this the same Nemesis who wants to cut us into little god pieces, stuff them into a cannon, and fire them at the moon?"

Before you encounter the Japanese Helper (only accessible at night) and learn the information he has regarding Nemesis, you need to convert the Japanese village that lies on the other side of the mountain near your Temple. This particular village is held by Nemesis and it will be your first direct confrontation with the game's big bad-guy god. As usual, you can send in your Creature to aid with the conversion process who by now should know a good array of villager-impressing Miracles. You can help out yourself by throwing objects (trees, rocks) or Fireballs from the mountain top.

When you eventually convert this Japanese village (and it shouldn't be too difficult at this stage), you activate the Swap To Bear Silver challenge plus a Gold Story Scroll in the forest nearby. Let's deal with the Gold Scroll first. Click on this and you are introduced to a rogue villager who is prepared to talk to you about life under Nemesis' rule. In a series of plot-advancing cutscenes, the Japanese Helper reveals that your Creature's power is being drained by a Wonder in one of the other opposing villages. The power of this Wonder is at its greatest at night.

This challenge is only accessible at night

SILVER SCROLL CHALLENGE 4
SWAP TO BROWN BEAR
REWARDS: Brown Bear Creature

"I refuse to get involved with this horrid challenge, Holy One. It's disgusting and unsanitary and eeeuuuchhh..."

"I used to have a job sweeping the neural pathways of the 'God of Having Last Night's Curry For Breakfast'. So this is nothing!"

Once the nearest Japanese village has been converted, the Silver Scroll that activates the Swap To Bear challenge appears over one of the huts. When clicked, a Japanese villager will inform you that there's a terrible stench coming from the nearby forest. Thus begins the challenge, a treasure hunt of sorts, which invites you to locate and pick up lumps of poo. Yes, you did read that right. Nobody said that a god's work was glamorous.

The idea here is to zoom in close to the ground and locate the little brown parcels in question. Not only will you be able to see the lumps of poo on the ground (start at the edge of the forest that's furthest away from the village), you'll also be able to hear them. As an extra indicator, Lionhead have thoughtfully added buzzing flies to each little pile of droppings. Your reward for finding and disposing of all the scattered number twos (the latter happens automatically) is the opportunity to swap your Creature for a brown bear. They are far from difficult to locate—the forest isn't that big and once you have discovered the first one, the others appear in a diagonal line leading towards the sea. Check out the brown bear's stats in the Creature Comforts section of this guide.

Find these lumps of poo and you'll be able to swap your Creature for a brown bear.

GOLD SCROLL CHALLENGE
JAPANESE HELPER
REWARDS: None

"Nemesis is hurting our Creature—his curse seems to be powered by Wonders in his villages. We must destroy them."

"No, we should destroy... hey, wait a minute, what did you say? You want to use violence!? I'm the evil one remember."

Once you've taken the nearest Japanese village (the one with the Swap To Bear challenge in it), you need to turn your attention to the next one, shown in the picture here. Like Land Three, where every village conquered lowered one of the three pillars trapping your Creature, the villages here contain curse-powering Wonders which must be eliminated. This first one seems to be draining your Creature of its power. You can attempt to attack it from a distance, but it's far more effective to convert the village. To reach Nemesis on this map, you'll have to take it at some point anyway. If you do manage to gain the settlement, Nemesis will destroy the Wonder himself.

When the first part of the curse is dispelled, another Gold Scroll will appear above the Japanese Helper in the forest. Click on it again to hear the next part of the Land Five storyline. This time, the renegade villager will tell you about the second Wonder which has reversed your Creature's alignment. So, if he was originally a goody-two-shoes type, he is now an uncaring bad-ass, and vice-versa. Of course, you can counter these effects somewhat by using the Leashes of Compassion and Aggression.

With few Nemesis-owned villages left, the second Wonder can be found in

You must destroy the curse-powering Wonders.

GOLD SCROLL CHALLENGE
JAPANESE HELPER (Continued)
REWARDS: None

the Greek village shown on this page. Again, you can try to attack this Wonder from a distance, but Nemesis will quickly protect his threatened settlement with appropriate Shield Miracles. As you'll discover, this level slowly and unavoidably becomes a war of attrition as you attempt to turn the tide of Belief in Nemesis' remaining villages. When you finally manage to take this village from Nemesis, your angry opponent will destroy the Wonder himself so that you cannot use it to augment your own powers.

When this penultimate village has fallen, the third and final part of this sequence is activated. This time, however, you have nothing to worry about. The Japanese Helper brings both you and your Creature to a place of healing. Here, your Creature rids himself of the invisible influence that has possessed him since the start of this final land. Finally, a Heal Miracle Dispenser will appear in the hills in the middle of the island. Your next move is obvious— Nemesis has only one village left. He doesn't want to lose this last line of defence and Influence, and hopes to deter an attack by blasting the landscape with multiple Mega Blast Miracles.

THE FINAL BATTLE
REWARDS: None

"Look! Nemesis has an Aztec Wonder which increases the power of all aggressive Miracles. Let's be careful."

"It's too late. Nemesis should have blasted us on Land One. But now we're too big and too powerful for him."

By now only one town should be left under Nemesis' rule. The people here are fanatically zealous about their god, and they have built a Sun Temple to enhance the power of all aggressive Miracles. This settlement is the hardest to take and you have to chip away at the Belief total while keeping hold of all your other villages. Gods are supposed to be everywhere at once. This is a true test of that ability. You'll only be able to mount a serious challenge here if you have built up your power, have trained your Creature well and have summoned crowds of worshippers to the Worship Site. When you finally manage to convert this Aztec stronghold, you'd be forgiven for thinking that the game is all but over. Nemesis, however, has a couple more tricks up his ethereal sleeve. The first of these is to transform his Creature into a mirror of your own, and to send it against you in battle. Use a combination of queued punches and Special Moves to defeat him. After this, you can elect to obliterate Nemesis' Temple in an attempt to wipe him out of existence. The game ends when you guide your Creature to the nearby volcano to fuse the three Creeds. You can either heal your Creature or just leave him. By the time you have got this far, there's nothing more that this part of the guide can tell you.

CHAPTER 6
MULTIPLAYER & SKIRMISH

"i am become death, shatterer of worlds."

Robert J. Oppenheimer, 1945

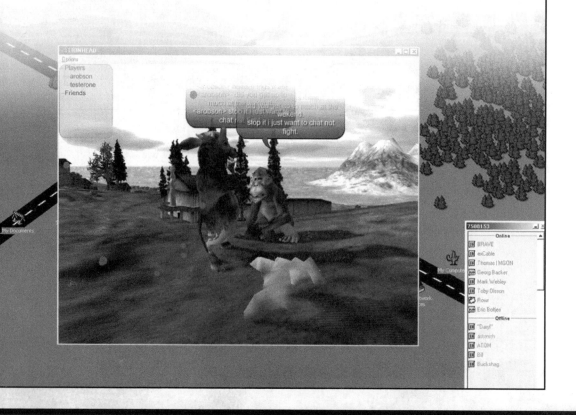

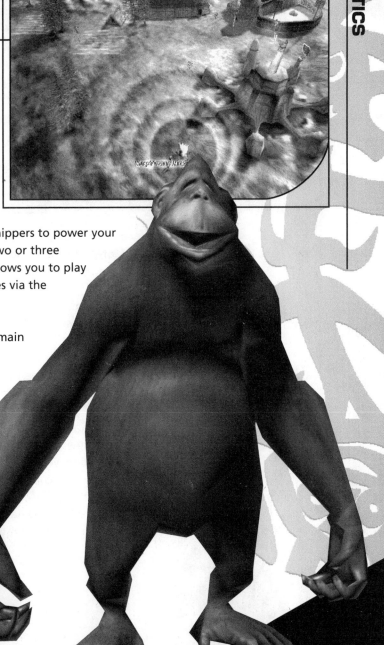

The more Belief you have, the more power you can wield.

On multiplayer and skirmish maps, speed and power is often more important than a fancy, complex village infrastructure. Not only must you actively micro-manage a series of villages, but you must balance this task against the need for expansion, for your own security and for bands of worshippers to power your Miracles. Skirmish pits you against one, two or three computer-controlled gods. Multiplayer allows you to play against numerous player-controlled deities via the Internet or Local Area Network (LAN).

Tactics here are much the same as in the main Story Mode. Boil down *Black & White's* gameplay, view it in a purely militaristic way, and your aim should be the pursuit of people. Think of them as fuel. The more villagers who bow down before you, the more you can summon to your Worship Site, and the quicker you can cast your Miracles. And the more villages you own, the wider the array of Miracles that you have at your disposal. Finally, *where* you expand is just as important as

Make sure you cast your Miracles to a crowd.

why. Chances are, you'll quickly develop a favourite Miracle, and you'll want to take a village that provides it. On skirmish and multiplayer maps, the drive to get a Worship Site built and running is greater than ever.

Once your empire begins to swell, it can become much more difficult to keep track of your people and how they are faring. Fortunately, using the TAB key, you can soar to the Village Store in each one of the villages that you own. Yet even with this handy shortcut and *Black & White's* Bookmarking function, you still need to have a presence in multiple settlements.

Or do you? Take time to study the methods employed by an opposing computer AI and you'll see that most of its satellite villages are left almost empty, the majority of their citizens busy at the Temple's Worship Site. It's a good illustration that a god is nothing without Prayer Power and an arsenal of Miracles. On any map with several neutral villages, it's tempting to expand quickly and to perhaps overextend your reach. In *Black & White*, your power comes from the people. No matter how many villages you control, you should never lose sight of this basic fact. More importantly, your villagers won't live for ever—you need to make sure that you have youngsters coming in as the old start to check out. In short, a constant supply of power.

MAP: Skirmish 1 (Two-Player)

MAP: Skirmish 2 (Three-Player)

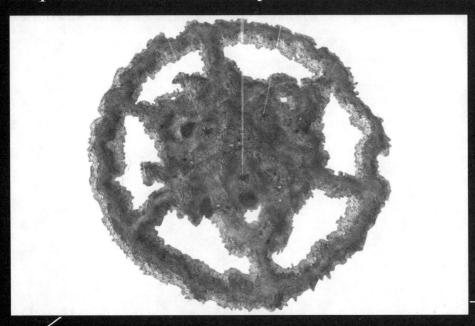

MAP: Skirmish 3 (Four-Player)

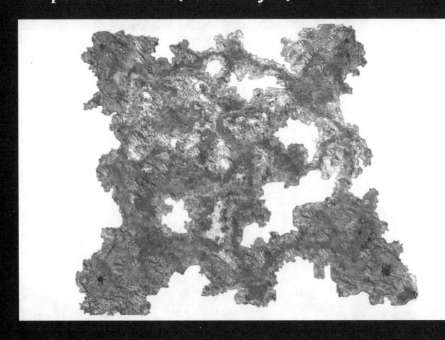

Tips & Tactics

The Skirmish and Multiplayer options require only a slightly different slant to the gameplay that you've been used to in the Story Mode. As such, the basic organisational tasks that you need to complete are much the same. At the start of a new multiplayer or skirmish game, the villagers in your home settlement will auto-divide into farmers, fisherman, builders and so on. Your first task should be to speed up the construction of your Worship site. Your second should be to send your Creature away to convert extra villages and expand your empire.

Once the Worship Site has been constructed, you'll need to set up your village to operate as efficiently as possible. You'll want to summon the majority of the inhabitants to provide Prayer Power, leaving only a skeleton crew of disciples to keep the village ticking over. Assign Farmer and Forester Disciples—make these all female and designate one Farmer per two fields. Set one young male villager to be a Breeder disciple and then set the Totem to between 70 and 80 percent to summon the villagers to the Worship Site.

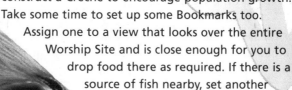

In your base village, you should have instant access to a Workshop and you should attempt to supply this with enough wood so that you can construct a Crèche to encourage population growth. Take some time to set up some Bookmarks too. Assign one to a view that looks over the entire Worship Site and is close enough for you to drop food there as required. If there is a source of fish nearby, set another Bookmark there allowing you to quickly transport fish to the Village Store. To take care of your worshippers, you'll need access to

Send women to work in the fields rather than to worship.

Planting Crop
A:24 L:93% F:58%

Planting Crop
A:29 L:90% F:61%

Going To Farm
A:33 L:96% F:49%

Planting Crop
A:24 L:89% F:92%

Food and Heal Miracles. If these don't come as standard with your basic home village, look around for one that *does* provide them. Finally, if there are no buildings to construct, don't forget to reassign the Builder Disciples you used to erect the Worship Site.

For the best insight into the multiplayer side of the game, who better to ask than the people at Lionhead? Game experts Andy Robson and Joe Borthwick are *Black & White* gods who are prepared to impart their empire-building wisdom to us mere gameplaying mortals.

ANDY ROBSON, GAMEPLAY AND TESTING

A combination of mouse and keyboard controls gives you the flexibility to move quickly around the gameworld. While you can use the mouse-wheel (if you have one) to zoom the view in and out, you get a better and faster response by using both mouse buttons. You can also use CTRL and SHIFT to zoom the view close in to your godly hand.

Your first task in any situation should be the completion of your Worship Site. If you're going to get anywhere in *Black & White*, you need quick access to the basic Miracles—Water for your fields and trees, plus Wood and Food. The Worship Site will be auto-planned and auto-built whenever you take over a village. Provide wood and a pile of food at the building site to save your builders a long walk for their materials. While the Worship Site is being constructed, designate your Disciples—a couple of Farmers (I make them all women), a male Breeder, plus a couple of Fishermen if appropriate. Forget about Foresters to begin with—it's quicker to simply pick up trees and deposit them either in the Workshop or the Village Store.

When the Worship Site is constructed, assign half of your population there straight away. This will ensure that you get some Prayer Power flowing in which can be used to charge up your Miracles. Disciples won't be affected by your religious call, and will work single-mindedly until you relieve them of duty. It's worth noting that by raising the Totem to 100 percent you can call everyone to the Worship Site, including Disciples. Take advantage of this feature to Heal your villagers and to prolong their life.

Obviously, your strategy is determined by what you start with. Long term, you should aim to build all of the civic buildings (Workshop, Crèche, Graveyard) and to construct a Wonder to enhance your Miracle-casting. The size of a Wonder is directly affected by the amount of Belief that you have in the village building it. A Wonder not only powers up your Miracles (see Chapter 3), but it also increases your Influence on the map. If you've taken the time to produce an Artefact and it is filled with Prayer Power (it will pulse with your colour), building a Wonder next to it will increase the size of the resulting building. After this, your Artefact can be moved—place it in an opposing village to aid in its conversion.

How high do you raise your Totem? 50 percent? 75 percent?

Once you have constructed all of the civic buildings (including the Wonder), you'll have the opportunity to build One-shot Miracle Dispensers. These are useful for enhancing your offensive and defensive capabilities. For example, you could place a Water Miracle Dispenser in a village to put out fires.

Where does your Creature fit in to all this? If you're playing a skirmish game you can use the same beast that you've been developing in the main Story Mode. Ideally, your Creature can be taught to do all of the rudimentary tasks that you won't have time to do—the provision of food and wood, adding to the supplies in the Village Store and so on. Your Creature exists to serve you, not to run around on his own doing whatever he feels like. Leash your Creature to a Desire pole in a village and he will look after that desire.

Villages should be able to tick over without much input from the player, thereby allowing you to concentrate on other things. You can always leash your creature to the Village Store and leave him to look after the village while you replant trees, cast spells, and erect new buildings elsewhere. You can also build new villages to bridge the gap between a village that you control and an opposing/neutral village that is too far away to reach easily. Creating new towns extends your Influence, and adds more people and Belief.

There are several other things that you could try:

- Replant trees in close proximity to create forests.
- Place rocks next to houses in your village to encourage Fireflies to hide underneaththem at night.
- Get your Creature to eat enemy villagers.
- Press "S" to keep track of the Age, Life and Food stats of your villagers.

Your Creature can impress a village quicker than you.

- Leash your Creature (using the Leash of Aggression) to an enemy village to make him attack it. Clicking on buildings in the village will encourage the Creature to destroy them.
- You can catch Fireballs if you see them coming in.
- Use Teleports to cut journeys for your villagers—the more that they have to walk, the more that they become tired, old and ineffective. Note: Teleports require constant Prayer Power to maintain.

> **TIP**
> If you drop a charging Miracle back on the Miracles Hand, you'll regain the power.

Joe Borthwick, QA Designer

The best way to approach a village you want to control is to fulfil their desires shown on their storage pit. This can be done in two ways:

1. You, as the player, provide them with what they need. Take wood, for example. There is more than one way to provide wood, and to get Influence quickly you would have to use as many of them as possible. This could be done by casting a Wood Miracle in the Village Store or on top of an incomplete building. You can also throw trees, bushes and fences directly into the Village Store. You have to use these different ways because villagers will soon become bored of seeing the same techniques. So it's important that you try to get as many people as possible in that village to see you doing these impressive tricks and miracles.

2. Use your Creature. The Creature can do anything you can and he has his own source of Prayer Power. This means that he can impress people quicker and also wander into areas that you are unable to reach (i.e. that are outside your Influence). Your Creature is an important tool when you want to impress a village, and, like you, he can gain Belief by doing both good and evil deeds.

There are many ways in which you can "impress" a village. Typically, I will destroy an enemy building and then supply wood to that same building. You'll gain influence for: (a) destroying the building and (b) helping the villagers rebuild it.

It also helps immensely to cast as many Miracles as possible because you, as a player, will gain Influence/Belief for every one you cast. The amount of Influence/Belief you get for casting a Miracle in front of a village will decrease the more you cast it—this is because villagers get bored of seeing the same thing time and time again. It's also important to use your Creature (a towering Miracle himself) to supply the village with the resources that it needs. As your Creature develops, he will eventually be able to tell villagers stories or dance for them. When he does this he will gather them together in one place. This is the best time for you to cast key Miracles. You get more Belief for Miracles if more people are there to witness them. There is little point in burning a house that has half the village in it because once they are dead, it becomes harder to impress that village.

There is one way around the people problem pointed out above: make your villagers into Missionaries and supply them to the village you want to gain. This will increase the population, which in turn means that there will be more villagers to impress. The more villagers you can impress, the quicker you can gain the settlement.

But while the Missionary angle sounds perfect in theory, there is a downside. If you supply your villagers to a village, a rival god can also gain Influence by impressing the new arrivals. You can avoid this for the most part by creating a diversion. Distract a rival player/god by sending your Creature into their territory in search of a fight. Whether he wins or loses is irrelevant. As the enemy is concentrating on the battle, you can begin to impress the village without worrying that you are competing with another god.

I have found that the best way to defeat another Creature is to use your Creature's Special Move. This is achieved by casting a gesture in the shape of a star. It's a devastating move and can be quickly followed by a hard hit to the opponent Creature's head. The idea is to use your own Creature's abilities to your advantage. Each player has an individual Creature (in terms of size, strength and speed), so each battle is unique. To stack the odds in my favour, I make sure that my Creature is around 80 percent strong and 40 percent fat. This ensures that he's hefty enough to take (and give) a few punches and be fast enough to avoid getting hurt.

Spells are also useful in Creature combat, but against an experienced player they won't be very effective. As you prepare to unleash a Miracle, the opponent's Creature will lash out at your Creature to interrupt the casting. There is also little point in queuing too many hits on an opponent's Creature, because as soon as your pattern is interrupted your Creature is left vulnerable, i.e. he will continue to try and hit the opposing Creature until all the "hit" points have been attacked.

Lastly, a quick word on supplying food to your villagers: New players can often find this a problem, but food is the last thing on my list of priorities when playing *Black & White*. This is because my strategy here involves making Farmer Disciples and allowing them to grow crops. I will then expand the village until I have constructed every building. Only then will I think about adding extra fields. They are expensive to make (four Scaffolds) and there are several reasons why you shouldn't bother.

> **TIP**
> If a Village has no people to impress, it can be taken over by placing followers into it or destroying it utterly.

1. You can cast food Miracles into the village store.
2. Your Creature can cast food Miracles into the village store.
3. You can throw cattle, sheep and pigs into the village store.
4. You can plunder the fish farms and throw up to 1,500-worth of food into the village store.

If I need to supply my village with food, I tend to summon the majority to the Worship Site and then supply the food there. When they are all satisfied, you can then add food to the Village Store. If possible, I try to have around 8-10 Fields to supply food for 50 people. That's about one field for every five people in the settlement. I always have a few Farmer Disciples and make sure that the fields are well watered. By teaching your Creature to water the crops, you can relieve yourself of this tedious but essential duty. Good irrigation will make the crops grow faster.

"I think that's everything. Village maintenance to the Story Mode walkthrough in one handy guide. It's been a pleasure guiding you through, Leader. I hope that you've learnt some new things..."

"I'd like to stay and chat, Boss. But I've got this hot date tonight with a Cherub. And I kinda invited her here to this page... So could you and, uh, Beardy give us a little space? Just close the book will ya! I'll see you in the sequel..."